ICTs, Community Access and Development

ICTs, Community Access and Development

Case Studies from Six Developing Countries

International Telecommunication Union

AAKAR

ICTs, Community Access and Development:
Case Studies from Six Developing Countries

First Published 2010

ISBN: 978-93-5002-059-3 (Hb)

Published by
AAKAR BOOKS
28 E Pocket IV, Mayur Vihar Phase I, Delhi 110 091
Phone: 011-2279 5505 Telefax : 011-2279 5641
aakarbooks@gmail.com; www.aakarbooks..com

Composed by
Limited Colors, Delhi 110 092

Printed at
Mudrak, 30 A Patparganj, Delhi 110 091

Contents

Abbreviations

ADSL – Asymmetric Digital Subscriber Line
AISI – African Information Society Initiative
APO – Agency Post Offices
BAAP – Buenos Aires Action Plan
BDT – Telecommunication Development Bureau (Bureau de Développement des Télécommunications)
CDMA – Code Division Multiple Access
CMC – Community Multi-Media Centre
CMO – Community Mail Offices
DGPT – Director General of Post and Telecommunication
ELSA – Evaluation and Learning System of Acacia
FAO – Food and Agriculture Organization
GPO – General Post Office
ICT4D – Information and Communication Technology for Development
IDRC – International Development Research Centre
ILO – International Labour Organization
ITU – International Telecommunication Union
LTN – Light data Telecommunication Network
MARD – Ministry of Agriculture and Rural Development
MCI – Ministry of Culture and Information

MCT – Multi-purpose Community Telecentre

MINSA – Ministry of Public Health

MOD – Ministry of Defence

MoH – Ministry of Health

MoST – Ministry of Science and Technology

MPT – Ministry of Posts and Telematics

MSSRF – M. S. Swaminathan Research Foundation

NPA – Norwegian People's Alliance

PTIT – Post and Telecom Institute of Technology

RIPT – Research Institute of Posts and Telecommunications

SILAIS – Ministry of Public Health in Nicaragua created local integrated health systems

TCRA – Tanzania Communication Regulatory Authority

TELCOR – Telecommunication Regulatory Body

TPDF – Tanzania Peoples' Defence Forces

TTCL – Tanzania Telecommunications Company Limited

UNESCO – United Nations Educational, Scientific and Cultural Organisation

UNHCR – United Nations High Commission for Refugees

VAP – Valetta Action Plan

VNPT – Vietnam Posts and Telecommunications Corporations

VSAT – Very Small Aperture Terminal

WHO – World Health Organization

Foreword

As part of its overall objective of connecting the unconnected, over the last decade ITU has initiated a number of projects with the aim of providing access to information and communication technologies for rural communities. These projects have typically involved a number of national and international partners. This study presents an evaluation of some of the ITU initiatives for access to ICT for rural and remote economies and is borne out of the belief that a comparative study of the lessons learnt from different projects is necessary to consolidate the experience. In addition, the study addresses some of the empirical and theoretical issues related to the role of ICT in transformation of marginal economies. The basic ITU model for facilitating access to ICT for the people of remote and rural areas was to create Multipurpose Community Telecenters (MCTs) with telecommunication connectivity, equipped with modern IT instruments and accessories and trained staff. The projects typically targeted different target groups, depending on specific location. Different partners collaborated to adapt content to demonstrate the impact of ICTs on occupational sectors – agricultural extension workers, health workers, teachers etc.

The underlying objective was to develop models for the provision of ICTs to rural and remote areas. However, variations on the basic model occurred when MCT projects encountered different issues at different project sites in different countries. These differences actually offer a great opportunity to study two important and much less understood aspects related to ICT and social and economic development. These are: social and economic factors that influence the acceptance and utilisation of ICT, and how to best realise the role that ICT can play in the process of economic and social development of marginal economies.

This study focuses on ITU projects in six countries. The six countries provide interesting variations in socio-economic status and differing needs of the target groups concerned. The projects are in Mali (Timbuctu), Bhutan, Honduras, Vietnam, Nicaragua and Tanzania. The settings vary – they encompass marginal economies, marginal economies in transition and emerging economies. Some provide case studies in alternative mode of access and one project is explicitly dedicated to communities living in refugee camps.

A uniform questionnaire formed the basis for the information collected. The questionnaire focused on the socio-economic status of the villages served by MCTs and also users and non-users of the ICT facilities in those villages. This volume documents some of the initiatives, their implementation and the outcomes. The studies were conducted during the period 2005-2008, We have great pleasure in making it widely available and trust that it will useful for similar initiatives in other developing countries.

The study has been written by Pradosh Nath and Vishnu Mohan Calindi.*

January 2010 **Sami Al-Basheer Al Morshid**

Director, Telecommunication Development Bureau

International Telecommunication Union, Geneva

Pradosh Nath is Deputy Director, National Institute of Science, Technology and Development Studies (Council of Scientific and Industrial Research), New Delhi.

Vishnu Calindi is Coordinator of Rural Telecommunications, Telecommunication Development Bureau, International Telecommunication Union, Geneva.

Acknowledgements

This study is based on information collected on the basis of a uniform questionnaire in different projects. This task was carried out by the project staff in selected countries. It is because of their extraordinary efficiency that the mobilisation of information from different corners of the globe was possible. Besides the questionnaire, the authors had visited project sites in Vietnam and Bhutan, and interacted with the target villagers and project personnel on various issues related success and sustainability of MCT initiatives.

We are grateful to the staff of different organizations involved in these projects. In Bhutan we would like mention the contribution of Mr. Biswa for providing all assistance. Postmasters at Wangdue, Punakha, Paro, and Phuentsholling were forthcoming to enlighten us on the functioning of the mail despatch and telekiosks. Mr. Jamayang shared his hands-on experience in establishing Telekiosks in different post offices. Mr. Ilari Pohto, Mr. Tandi Wangchuk, Mr. Jigme Tenzin, Mr. Amar Pradhan, to name a few, enriched our understanding of the project in the social and economic milieu of Bhutan. We take this opportunity to express our gratitude to all of them.

The present volume has given a special attention to the concept of 'Cultural Points' as a unique way of organising ICT services for remote and rural areas in Vietnam. We are grateful to Dr. Phung Van Van, President of PTIT who explained the finer social and economic aspects of the concept of 'Cultural Points' in Vietnam. We are also thankful to Ms. Dinh Thi Thu Phong, Ms. Quan Duy Ngan Ha and Mr. Lee Thai Hong, Mr. Ngo Van Thuc, Mr. Vo Thanh Nam and Mr. Nguyen Thai Ha, and Mr. Nguyen Ngoc Son.

Dasho Meghraj Gurung (Bhutan), Mr. Birama Diallo (Mali), Mr. Roger Aguirre (Honduras and Nicaragua), Mr. Julian Massawe (Tanzania) prepared the country reports based on the information collected through the questionnaire. Mr. Roberto Bastidas, the Head of the ITU Area Office in Tegucigalpa, Honduras and the moving spirit behind the Honduras and Nicaragua projects, provided invaluable assistance. We owe a debt of gratitude to all of them for sharing their insights and their incisive comments on the earlier draft.

This study would not have been possible without the help of many ITU colleagues. We owe special debt of gratitude Yuri Grin, Emamgholi Behdad, Riccardo Passerini, Marcelino Tayob, Brahima Sanou, Margarida Evora-Sagna, and Lucy Macdermot. We thank Nicolas Stauble and Simon De Nicola for designing the cover page. We are grateful to Sami Al-Basheer Al-Morshid, Director of BDT for his encouragement.

Disclaimer: The opinions expressed in this report are those of the authors and do not necessarily represent the views of the International Telecommunication Union (ITU) or its membership. The designations employed and the presentation of material, including maps, do not imply the expression of any opinion whatsoever on the part of ITU U concerning the legal status of any country, territory, city or area, or concerning the delimitations of its frontiers or boundaries. The mention of specific companies or of certain products does not imply that they are endorsed or recommended by ITU in preference to others of a similar nature that are not mentioned.

Introduction

ICT and underdevelopment: An empirical investigation

A group of interrelated technologies (electronic devices) for accessing, processing and disseminating information is called Information and Communication Technologies (ICTs). ICTs are important technological means to help utilize information for the transformation of rural and remote economies (together they are called marginal economies) . The obvious first step is to make ICTs available to the marginal communities. Community Telecentres are a popular means of reaching the marginal communities in rural and remote areas. There are various national and international agencies which are promoting programmes for setting up Community Telecentres in different countries in Africa, Asia, and Latin America. These Telecentres address the issues related to poverty alleviation, education, health, gender issues and governance. Problems relating to sustainable development through access and wider application of ICT remained the major concern of the Community Telecenter Projects. These Telecentres are typically equipped with a telephone, a PC with dial-up connection for internet, a fax machine, and in some cases a scanner. Administration and management of such telecentres vary from direct involvement of the government departments to the ones run by local communities.

There are various perspectives of the efficacy of Telecentres. Colle and Roman (2003) suggest that a Telecentre is 'a shared facility that provides public access to information and communication technologies'. According to Zongo (1999) of the IDRC's Acacia programme, a telecentre "is a place where public access to communication and information for economic, social and cultural development is provided through IT". Kanfi and Tulus (1998) define a telecentre as "a location which facilitates and encourages the provision of a wide variety of public and private information-based goods and services, and which supports local economic or social development."

How did these Telecentres perform? Are there any noticeable impacts on the economic and social lives of the target communities? Telecenter experiments have generated a few interesting debates. All reviews, both empirical and theoretical, unanimously indicate that ICT, as a tool alone cannot be expected to either alleviate poverty or remove social anomalies. Awareness, education, skill development, and creating relevant information content are essential ingredients to make ICT perform its expected role (Brown, 2001). To make any visible impact the Telecentre programme has to be coupled with other social and economic development programmes that create opportunities for livelihoods (Hudson, 2001).

Sustainability of the Telecenters beyond the project life (or once the institutional funding comes to an end) remains a major concern. The question of sustainability of the community telecenter project has thrown up issues with wider implications. Fuchs (1998b) and others argue for public funding of the centres, as a "public good" similar to libraries and schools. Richardson (1998, 2002) suggests that these projects should be run by self-sustaining entrepreneurs – anything else encourages incompetence and dependency. He strongly argues in favour of commercially run telecom services. According to him, there is enough demand for telecom services in rural areas, and what is needed is judicious study of the nature of demand and preparing the regulatory framework accordingly. According to Opoku-Mensah (1998) "Their sustainability depends on them being run on business lines and charging enough money to users to keep the operation sustainable. That may not be a bad thing but perhaps they should call a spade a spade and not raise expectations that these services will be affordable to everyone". Ernberg (1998a) differentiates the need and demand for telecentres. He argues that there is very little demand (as opposed to need) for telecentres in rural areas, as economic demand requires people both to have money and to perceive a benefit for themselves in the telecentre. In a critical note, Colle and Roman (1999) observed that the potential contribution of ICTs to rural development is an assumption or a belief and it is yet to be proved. In many telecentre projects, it is assumed that providing the ICT equipment will automatically make the useful information available to those who want it.

In simplest words, the problem of sustainability is the balance between the revenue earned over the cost of running such centres. Not enough revenue earned implies the following:

(i) Lack of demand for the services provided by the centres. This may be due to an inappropriate content of the services, and lack of awareness of the target population. Lack of demand could be because of the lack of economic activities in the target region; and

(ii) Prices of the services are beyond the affordability of the non-users of the services among the target population.

Both these issues have been highlighted by different evaluation reports of the telecenter projects (Latchman and Walker, 2001). The question of sustainability, however, does not question the relevance of the project; instead it indicates the need for better understanding of the best practices for taking the ICT to the services of the people of the marginal economies (Anderson, 1999). In the context of the emerging technological scenario of decreasing cost of connectivity, the Chairman of the United Nations ICT Task Force observed, "If the world recognizes that knowledge is power, and there is no excuse for the enormous cost associated with providing access to information, then we now have an obligation to use these information kiosks as a tool for advancement" (Figueres, 2003). This view has been echoed while justifying the projects financed by infoDev programme of the World Bank. It says, "....evidence is now sufficient to affirm that information technology, telecommunications and connectivity, in general, are significant contributors (and in some regards pre-requisites) to poverty reduction." "The time has now come to gather, compare and combine the many successful experiences of such centres and kiosks around the world, to identify best practices, and to encourage and support their replication and their dissemination" (Lanvin, 2003). Therefore, the main concern for sustainability is to make the Telecentres access-worthy through understanding, and developing the locally relevant, useful and affordable content. This can be achieved through carefully consolidating the lessons learnt from the ongoing projects across the globe. But this consolidation is not an easy task, particularly when dealing with communication and its contribution to the transformation of marginal economies.

As Roman and Colle (2003) observed, "Telecenters remain largely an atheoretical area of research. However, to rigorously tackle the problems described above, research requires a strong theoretical base". The absence of a generally acceptable theoretical perspective takes away the rigour from the performance evaluation of the telekiosk projects and, as a result, a large number of evaluation reports that are available provide neither any substantive critical appraisal/evaluation, nor comparability of different initiatives. Many of them are anecdotes describing the beneficial impact of ICTs on the welfare of the community or region (Barbet et al 2001). The question that remained unanswered is: can we evaluate the performance of the telecentres to suggest that they have lessened the level of poverty among the target population, or reduced gender discrimination?

The present volume arrives at the question through a somewhat different route. We begin with the question: what is the distinction between those who seek and use information and those who do not? If Telecentres were expected to bring the non-users into their fold, these distinctive factors would help in identifying the pre-requisites of the telecentre projects and also the criteria for their performance evaluation. The International Telecommunication Union (ITU) initiatives in this regard through its Multipurpose Community Telecentre (MCT) project provide an opportunity to address the question. We, therefore, begin with a conceptual note on the role information plays in social and economic lives, and suggest crucial socio-economic variables that get affected and do influence the extent and nature of information used in a given social and economic system. This volume has been planned based on studies carried out on the ITU initiatives of creating ICT infrastructure through MCT to serve the rural and remote areas in some of the Asian, African and Latin American countries. Regarding the ITU initiatives of MCT pilot projects, Ernberg (1998) observed "to this end pilot projects are implemented in a number of countries in different regions, at different stages of development and with different geographical, social, economic and cultural conditions". This provides an opportunity to examine telecentres in the light of highly diversified social and economic scenarios.

Therefore, theoretical perspective and a clearly defined methodology are the prerequisites for evaluation studies of the telecentre projects. In this volume an effort has been made to suggest a contour of a theory and methodological clarity derived out from the evaluation of telecenter projects of ITU in six different countries. The study covered five MCTs in Honduras, four in Vietnam, two in Nicaragua, two in Tanzania, eight in Bhutan, and one in Mali. The study is divided into eight chapters:

- The first chapter deals with the theoretical and methodological issues. The theoretical contour suggests the role of information in the transformation of an economy from a marginal to the take-off stage. The issue of economic transformation is treated by choosing cases that represent various stages.
- In the second chapter, the experience of MCT at Timbuctu in Mali is presented as a case of a marginal economy.
- The third chapter takes up the case of Bhutan, a shade different from Mali in terms of literacy and economic stability.
- The MCTs in Honduras, as presented in chapter four, are the case where lack of economic opportunities has wasted the advantage of high rate of literacy.
- On the other hand, Vietnam could synchronize the social and economic development programme with the spread of ICT for achieving high rate of economic growth. The case of Vietnam is presented in the fifth chapter.
- The sixth chapter presents the pro-active state of Nicaragua in bringing the benefits of ICT to the people of rural and remote areas. The case of Nicaragua is

presented as an argument that for a population which is uninitiated and yet to be ICT ready, the direct role of the state and various governmental departments in addressing the needs of the community appears to be an important alternative.

- The seventh chapter is about the MCT services in the refugee camps of Tanzania, where ICT serves for the much needed social interactions among the homeless and stateless people of the refugee camps.
- The last chapter concludes with an overall summation of lessons learnt from the MCT projects on the role of information in economic and social development and highlights the need for differential services based on the status of the economy/society and the cause to be served.

1

Contours of an Approach for Performance Evaluation

Information and Development

Any social and economic analysis is flawed if it begins with the assumption that all the actors in an economy/society have equal access to information. The issue, however, does not disappear by ensuring equal access, because equal access does not ensure equal ability to utilize the same information by all the actors. Even after getting access, the use of information may be hindered by poor infrastructure, high prices, ignorance or illiteracy (Hudson, 1984; Heeks, 1999; Wresch, 1996). Once equal access is ensured, different actors may access different sets of information at different points of time and make different senses out of the accessed information and may decide to take actions of entirely different nature. Having access, accessing, and making sense out of accessed information are three different acts with widely different implications. Accessing and making sense of information is an intended action on the part of the actors in the society. If the intended action is called the enterprise of the actor, the nature of action (consequent to making sense of information) depends on the level of general awareness of the actor. Both formal and informal education shapes the general awareness, and, therefore, is indispensable for realization of the role of information in economic and social development. This is a non-figurative definition of demand for information.

The supply of information is like air. It is ubiquitous. We do not know when, where, what and how much of it we are using. Leaving this costless aspect aside, the supply of information is constituted in packaged form that addresses a perceived demand of information of various types and nature. This is the demand of an articulate market described above. Following Cassan (1997) we can state that in such an economy, information is the most critical input for decision-making for the coordination of large number of economic actors involved in production, services and exchanges. Seen this way, we can postulate that the greater the need for coordination and higher the complexity of decision making, the greater is the demand for information. When coordination/decision-making is regarding catching-up with or outdoing others (as it is in a typical competitive situation), seeking privileged access to information sets the dynamics of demand for information. The whole spectrum of the information market, therefore, is constituted of costless information (accessible to everybody) at one end, and high price information (exclusion principle) at the other. The latter corresponds to the economic system with adequately developed markets, while the former one is the economy/society where activities are defined by traditional wisdom; changes are rare and the need for information is rarely felt. These are the marginal economies. By marginal economies or communities we mean economies or societies that predominantly show the characteristics of a subsistence economy, negligible externalization of the economic activities, and insignificant individual initiatives to graduate to skill-based and knowledge-based economic activities. Such economies are essentially dependent on age-old farming practices. In terms of broad economic indicators, these economies will have a high level of poverty, low productivity, and poor economic and social infrastructure.

Information and Underdevelopment

The above description draws a broad distinction between underdeveloped (marginal) and developed economies in terms of information intensity; or let us call it the extent of informatization. It has been argued that the distinction between the information 'haves' and 'have-nots' is the basis for the dichotomies between the developed and developing, and the rich and poor – an information perspective of underdevelopment (Zijp, 1994). The journey from a marginal state of an economy to a developed economy is associated with a higher degree of informatization. However, the cause and effect relationship between the two is complex. The imminent question arises: is there any evidence that the prosperity of marginal economies is being hindered by the absence of access to information? There are two possible types of responses to the question. First, there are sceptics who would say that one does not survive by eating or drinking information. Much of the problem of the less developed world of Africa, Latin America, and Asia is the lack of two square meals a day. Sceptics are not sure if access to information helps earning two square meals for the barely-fed children of Somalia (Brown, 2001, Chowdhury, 2000). Secondly, there are positivists who think that the association is unquestionable. Information technology has changed the material world; it would also change social and economic lives, both in the developed and the less developed world. As Castells (1998, 1999) argued, "Information technology, and the ability to use it, is the critical factor in generating and accessing wealth, power and knowledge in our times... The disinformation of Africa at the dawn of the Information Age may be the most lasting wound inflicted in this continent by new patterns of dependency." In this context two recent publications entitled *ICT Infrastructure in Emerging Asia: Policy and Regulatory Roadblocks* (Samarajiva and Zainudeen, 2008), and *Digital Review of Asia Pacific,*

2007–2008 (Orbicom -IDRC, 2008) may be cited. We would like to have an elaborate review of the two books because together these two publications capture both critical optimism and uncritical zeal for ICTization and development as could be seen in the literature on this subject during the last decade. Read together, the two books reveal the strengths and weaknesses of the access to ICT programmes. The first book is on regulatory issues that are expected to work as enablers to ICT penetration in the developing and less-developed countries. The discussion on regulatory issues is preceded with articles based on a survey of demand for ICT services among the people living at the bottom of pyramid (BOP) in the socio-economic structure, and also by various types of people's initiatives to create access through innovative technical and organisational arrangements as have been observed in the much discussed success story of the 'Grameen Bank' in Bangladesh and various community actions in Indonesia. The second book on the other hand, is a status report on digital divide in the Asia Pacific. The book is divided into two distinct parts. The first part discusses the issues related to ICT4D in the countries in Asia Pacific region, while the second part reviews the ICT profiles of 31 countries in the region.

The concern for ICT infrastructure has been clarified in the introduction of the first book. Briefly, it is important because ICT enables communication in real time over the long distance. And communication being one of the important contributors to economic growth, (causation although is not yet fully understood), universal access to ICT is expected to enable the economic development of the emerging economies of Asia. It is also argued that the question of causation has become less important since private investment is gradually replacing the need for public funded development of the ICT infrastructure. Therefore, government involvement can be directed towards creating regulatory frameworks that would be conducive to bring in more and more private investment. The grey area, however, is the mis-match between the need and demand of the yet-to-be- reached segment of the population of the countries in emerging Asia. Also important is the possible mis-match between the interest of the private investment and developmental priorities of the welfare state. The discussion on regulatory issues, therefore, has to stand on the foundation of proven demand for communication (ICT) from those who remained unreached. The sections of the first book the have been structured accordingly; the first two sections assure that not only the people at the bottom of the pyramid are willing to spend for communication but it is also possible to make good business out of it. Two more sections that follow discuss the efficacy of different regulatory instruments generally in use in the emerging economies of Asia.

The basic argument that has been put forward through different contributions in the volume runs somewhat like this: access to ICT has to be extended up to the bottom of the pyramid (BOP)—meaning, to the bottom of the economic and social hierarchy. Be assured of the demand from the bottom. These studies have shown that BOP has higher marginal propensity to spend on communication compared to upper layer of the pyramid. They will connect more if some of the inconveniences are taken care of through competition among instrument and service providers. Much of this inconvenience is actually the result of an inappropriate regulatory regime that fails to eliminate entry barrier and pave the way for more and more private players. It is at this stage the central argument of the Book becomes quite confusing. The confusion reaches at its peak when we reach the last article in the Book titled'..... Through the market'. It says that market failure is the favourite excuse of the regulators. This study has discovered (reported in the three articles in the first section) that low income subscribers do not care about the price; they want reliable connectivity with privacy. It has also been discovered that they spend a higher proportion of their income for communication, which has been interpreted as huge unattended demand. For people at BOP spending on ICT is not entertainment, it is more of a compulsion that is opted after weighing it against time and labour that are as such quite abundant and valueless inputs for people at BOP.

The views in the second book, conspicuous by the absence of such blind zeal, are more balanced and wise. The book raises quite a few most pertinent issues; e.g. how is the access to ICT faring for development? If we compare certain key indicators, as provided in the second book, a few interesting observations emerge. The OECD countries in the Asia Pacific regions, like Japan and South Korea, have per capita GDP USD 36000 and 16000, respectively. These are accompanied with per hundred population 46 fixed and 74 mobile telephone connections in Japan and 57 and 79 for South Korea. Compare the same with Bangladesh (per capita GDP USD 482, 3 fixed and 2 mobile telephone connections per hundred population) or Lao (per capita GDP USD 490, 2 fixed and 13 mobile telephone connections per hundred population). The strong positive correlation between ICT penetration and status of the economies is well known. What intrigues researchers in this field is the ambiguity of the cause and effect relations between the two. As shown in the article by Sciadas, the existence of two Asias is a reality. The comparative picture of infodensity and infouse indicates the importance of the capacities of the countries to make use of the opportunities created by ICT. There are too many slips between ICT and development because the relations are not only non-linear, but they are also multi-dimensional and multi-directional, an issue totally missed in the articles of the first book. In their article Butt *et al* write, "The early

Internet dream that held e-commerce as the saviour of the artisan producer has not come to fruition, even though there have been well-promoted individual success stories. Instead, the rise of ICTs has brought unprecedented consolidation in markets. While there will always be success stories among the poor, there is no doubt that ICTs are, overall, increasing the gap between wealthy and poor business, countries and regions".

These understandings and concerns are not reflected in the discussion on regulatory issues presented in the first book that almost solicits a free hand to private operators, given substantial unmet demand from BOP. This, notwithstanding the discussions on 'smart subsidies', 'universal service obligation and the incumbent service provider', and also on the 'access deficit tax', provide valuable insights to the weaknesses of these regulatory instruments. The solution, however, is not in the free play of the private interest, particularly when it is regarding the hapless poor people at the BOP. In the second book, Butt *et al* observe, "There are indications that ultimately, specialization and focus on the non ICT path of society remain critical for successful ICT4D projects". This is regarding the capacity of the economy of BOP to make use of the opportunities that is expected to be created by the access to ICT, and social and economic complexities that are associated with it. Unlike Phongsathorn, Butt *et al* suggest, "Policy makers have to take stock of their true situation and resources available to them rather than following one-size-fits-all blueprints for ICT-enabled development".

Researchers and policy makers, reflecting upon experiences from various 'access to information' programmes, realise that what remains between information and social and economic development, is the arrangement for making information useable (Burlow, 1998).

Our argument here is that it is a wrong question to ask for understanding the relationship between information and economic development, as it is to ask how access to air contributes to economic and social development. The only difference between the two is that in the case of air, having access ensures its contribution, while in the case of information, access has to be coupled with ability to make sense and use of information. Use of information depends on the cognitive ability of human beings, but it is not so in the case of air. Information, in a marginal economy, works like air. Its access is non-exclusive; it has the same meaning to everybody. A marginal community accesses and uses the same information in the same sense. An individual's cognitive ability is subsumed in the cognitive ability of the community. Here, in terms of information content, community is not the sum of individuals; but is equal to each individual who is again equal to each other. All the individuals in the community hold the same information; they make the same sense out of it and, therefore, the sum of the individuals' information (knowledge pool) intensity is equal to one individual's information intensity, which is again equal to the information intensity of the whole community.

Education and exposure to the world outside the community enhance the cognitive ability of individuals. A Simonian individual[1] is different from other individuals in their respective abilities; not in terms of extent of limitedness, but in terms of types of cognition. Different individuals make different sense of the same information, and thus born individuals in a community. Therefore, the journey from marginal economy to developed economy is also a journey from community centric economic decisions to the emergence of individualized economic decisions resulting proliferation of individual enterprises. Economic activities become multi-dimensional, as becomes demand for information succinctly individualized, where individuals are no longer receivers of information[2]. They actively seek privileged access to information, and pay a price for its exclusivity.[3] With the proliferation of individual enterprises, the economy becomes more outward looking and multi-dimensional. There would be a gradual increase of exports and imports in the economy. Such economic changes would be accompanied by changes in social relations and practices.

Answer to the questions raised by sceptics is that providing two square meals to unfed millions, as a one-time problem, is easy. What is difficult is to make the same provision on a sustainable basis. And much more difficult is to initiate a dynamic process of economic development that would elevate the status of the society in question from a meagre two square meals to a standard of living of desirable comfort. The latter requires bringing the unfed millions into economic actions and also into the process of making and taking their own decisions. That is, when having access, accessing (as an intended act on the part of individual) and making sense of information plays a pivotal role in the process of economic and social development. Similar views were derived from the experience of ICT access programme in Africa. Okpaku (2006) argued that ICT infrastructure development and ICT for development are two interdependent but different propositions. The former does not automatically lead to the latter. The former deals with the delivery of services, and the other is about socio-economic wellbeing in the form of poverty reduction, political stability, and self actualization. Once such transformations take place, the demand for more and better services increases.

Information and Social Transformation

The marginal economies, as they are described above, are not those economies that are a few years behind the developed economies. It is actually a complex case of stunted development resulted from of multiple causes. This basically means that such economies will not evolve on their own way within a real time period. Therefore, efforts have been made to bring in changes in the economic and social practices through varieties of social and economic development programmes for skill development, local resource utilization, spread of modern education, etc. Similarly, a low level of information intensity of these economies is also a reflection of the same state of stunted growth, and is not likely to increase, on its own course without an external push.

Zembylas (2009) observed, "The issue is not about the importance of physical access but the lack of acknowledging first, the existing social and economic inequalities and power differentials that essentially subvert simplistic efforts to increase physical access between rich and poor communities. In other words, a redefinition of the way that digital divide is theorized is needed in both socio-political and pragmatic terms. A socio-political analysis of the digital divide encompasses questions about extent to which ICT locates the source of inequity and the traces left in people's lives or perpetuates those". A more critical observation and requirement of cautious approach to ICTization was the possibility of electronic colonization instead of the promise of inclusion (Zembylas and Vrasidas, 2005). In an earlier work, Warschauer (2003) expressed similar reservations about simplistic understanding of the issues of access to ICT, and suggested rethinking the understanding of digital divide and ways to narrow the divide. Valadez and Duran (2007) also echoed the same view and suggested that the reviews of many initiatives of the universal access programmes indicted the necessity of redefining the digital divide.

Setting up of the process of dynamic use of information in marginal economies has to be gradual and three-pronged. First is through creating appropriate access to information.

This means that it is to be geographically accessible to the target community, so that the target group of people do not have to struggle in terms of time and resources for having physical access to the information. The turn to transformation actually begins when the members of the community are persuaded to access and use new information. To begin with, the set of information (content) that they might take interest in would be the one that can improve their present economic plight. There has to be dedicated sites having content on developmental programme and opportunities through alternative economic and social practices. This will create access-worthiness of the sites for the members of the targeted marginal community. Mansell and When (1998) have argued that the capacity to generate and share information about local resources is as important as capacity to create access to ICT. The programme of universal education that has to be coupled with developmental programme gears the next turn to transformation. That is how will begin the act of sense making and individual centric decision-making. Members of the community in this process will gradually emerge as an information-seeking society from the earlier garb of information receiver. It is to be noted that content development plays critical role in initiating the marginal community to the world of information. Access to the content that is developed for the initiation has to come free to the marginal community, because it addresses the community's need (and not demand) as perceived by the developmental agencies. The transformation of the marginal community would be associated with the replacement of need by the demand for content with price attached.

Sustainability of Telecentres

How quickly can this transformation process be completed? The time taken will depend on the efficiency of the awareness development programme, appropriate content development, and also on achieving synthesis by integrating access to ICT with other economic and social development programmes such as skill development, resource utilisation, education, health, and hygiene (Jarboe, 2001). And the task is not easy. It has been argued by Schware (2005) that, "Although ICT-enabled projects can contribute greatly to the achievement of developmental goals, they are risky endeavours. Poorly designed projects can waste precious resources that could be devoted to competing development needs". According to Neto *et al* (2005), "To date, however, we know little about the impact of these technologies and it remains relatively difficult to evaluate the effectiveness of past and current practices in the field. This is in part because e-development is not an end in itself, but rather a process that uses modern ICT to increase productivity, trade and the delivery of services. In the end, the measure of success of ICT in development will not focus on the spread of technology, but on overall progress towards economic growth...."

Telecentres are projected interventions for creating access to ICT. As a tool for development, ICT cannot be a stand-alone means for uplifting marginal economies. Therefore, Telecentres have to synthesize their programmes with other developmental agencies. To accomplish this, it is necessary to "focus on the transformation, not the technology" (Jarobe, 2001; Warschauer, 2002).

As projected interventions, telecentres seek self-sustainability within projected life span. In most of the cases, life span of the project is determined on the basis of the availability of funding, and rarely on careful assessment of the time needed for achieving the transformation. Self-sustainability of telecentres depends on the extent of use of the services provided, which, in turn, depends on, as argued above, how the services are integrated with other developmental programmes. Ernberg (1998) argues that in the telecentre projects, the focus should shift from its own sustainability to making overall development initiatives that are sustainable through enrichment of the information and communication components.

Telecentres can earn self-sustainability only in a long drawn and round about way. In such projects, initially social benefits have to be greater than private benefits (in this case profit to the telecentres), and that is actually the justification of such projects. Gradually as the social benefits stabilize, it would have cascading effects in all other sectors, including the ICT sector, with the development of market for information. Therefore, life of the project (meaning funding the activities of the telecenters) has to be co-terminous with the transformation of the target economy, which would be indicated by the emergence of commercial incentives for providing ICT services. Any claim of sustainability or any attempt to gain sustainability before the transformation process is over would actually be spurious in the sense that sustenance is derived from other sources (or attending the demand of the non- have-nots) rather than from the projected one.

Another aspect of sustainability is the local human resource which would be able to address the technological issues associated with local needs. Such local needs are relevant for content development and also for technological solutions to hardware and software related problems, not to undermine the problems of maintenance, upgradation, troubleshooting and also training the users. Moyo (1996) had observed in his study on Africa that indigenous manpower development is a must to realize the long-term impact of ICTs for rural and remote area development.

Approaches Towards an Evaluation Methodology[4]

It may be noted here that ICT is an important tool, because information is considered to be an essential component of economic and social development. Or, in other words, access to information is considered to be an important tool against many economic and social anomalies. Any discussion on ICT, therefore, has to be built around the understanding of the complex role of information in society and economy; ICT being just incidental, a technological means of making information available in real time irrespective of the space of origin of the information. It is also to be noted that use of information cannot be streamlined or anticipated and exhausted. So is the impact of ICT on development, which has both-way relationship, and simultaneously impact each other. Cause and effect relationship between the two is not straightforward. Therefore, Changes in the socio-economic parameters cannot be directly attributed to the changes in the extent of use of ICT.

The ACACIA programme of IDRC is a comprehensive initiative to take ICT to the poor and underprivileged in selected African countries. The programme is built on partnership of African governments and international organizations under the African Information Society Initiative (AISI). The initiative takes a long term perspective of meeting the existing disparities in ICT infrastructure of African countries with respect to developed countries and aims to "demonstrate particularly how disadvantaged groups and communities can be empowered to solve the local development problems through the use of information and communication". Access to ICT, in this programme, has an accompanying two-pronged strategy of integrating it with information on the national level developmental initiatives through innovative technical infrastructure and equipment and, on the other hand, developing capabilities among the target population and improving public information delivery. The programme was initiated in 1997 and focused on the countries of Mozambique, Senegal, South Africa and Uganda. A continuous assessment system was in place through the Evaluation and Learning System of Acacia (ELSA). The first phase of establishing telecentres was done in partnership with UNESCO, ITU and national governments.

The IDRC evaluation studies bring out certain interesting aspects related to dynamics of the use of ICT among the target population. For initiating and managing such projects of mediating access to information and activating the social and economic life of underprivileged through access to ICT, the centres have to take the target community along for understanding and articulating its needs and developing suitable contents accordingly. The evaluation studies also indicate that factors like age, gender, education and economic status define the user pattern of the ICT and information.

The studies by UNESCO report about bringing in substantial participation and changes in the quality of life of the target communities through equitable and expanded access to ICTs. The UNESCO studies say, " Longer term benefits are already being realized within individual communities, such as the gradual removal of barriers to social inclusion, the stimulation of poverty alleviation through access to knowledge of better health, resource management and agriculture practices through the establishment of listeners clubs as self help groups (a direct connection between Community Multi-media Centre (CMC) work and the generation of income from small savings and credit operations), and the creation of new livelihoods opportunities." There is a cautionary note with the evaluation that reads, "While the evaluation team has concluded that the CMCs pilots are serving their communities well, it is difficult to attribute this success entirely to the UNESCO initiative. All CMCs in the pilot programme were created through the addition of a technology or service to an existing facility that has had a variety of investments from the community and other donors."

Along with many other initiatives to reach the information have-nots, two distinctive but equally important issues are thrown up. One is the Telecentre's best practices for sustainable and replicable models of ways to provide access to modern telecommunication facilities and information services, particularly to people in rural and remote areas (Ernberg, 1998a). Things to be considered, as listed by McConnell *et al* (2001) include:

(i) Technical issues: Basic infrastructural requirements and systems development (telephones, electricity, and telecom service providers), also availability and responsiveness of technical support and expertise.

(ii) Institutional issues: Locating a telecentre within the existing institutional framework and building on existing knowledge networks (formal and informal), i.e. in partnership with local government schools, libraries, universities, etc. and civil society organizations.

(iii) Economic issues: Income generation, cost recovery, ability to pay, participatory market demand assessments to identify optimal location of information services.

(iv) Social and cultural issues: Information content and format appropriate to the context of users, capacity of managers/operators of information services to identify and supply the information needs of users, and human capacity (literacy, numeracy) of beneficiaries to make use of information.

(v) Political: Participation in planning and implementation, political networks, local power relations and in access, discrimination and exclusion.

The other issue is the evaluation of the actual social and economic benefits expected to be generated through these projects. Michiels and Van Crowder (2001), in a review of

ICT-based initiatives, point out that impact of these projects on economic and social livelihoods of the target communities is very little understood. Gomez *et al* (1999) wrote, "Until relevant methodologies and adequate tools are developed to effectively assess the social impact of the application of ICTs for sustainable development from the user's perspective, efforts to demonstrate how people are empowered by knowledge will lack credibility".

Some valuable insights, in this regard, are available from the ACACIA programme of IDRC focused on Africa. The programme had an in-built arrangement of continuous learning based on detailed documentation of the experience of the project staff. The consolidated report brings out many important social and economic dimensions of the use and non-use of ICT-facilitated access to information by the target communities who are poor and underprivileged.

Millar has done an extensive review of the major trends in evaluation frameworks and methodologies. The major trends identified are as follows:

Whole system approach

As opposed to a linear system of cause and effect relationship, this approach pays more attention to the dynamics of socio-economic transformation involving ICTs. The approach avoids a technology determinist perspective and examines the use of ICT for creating economic value (Mansell *et al*, 1998). Daly (1999) followed this approach to assess the impacts of Internet use and non-use in Africa and to capture the inter-relationships between the 'penetration' and 'utilization' of the Internet and its effects on individuals, groups and communities.

The main problem with the frameworks as discussed is that while claiming to be holistic, they focus mainly on penetration of ICT. Even to be ignored, the causality aspect between ICT and development has to be understood. What is to be shunned is mono-causality. The frameworks assume that the impact of ICT (once spread) is automatic. This is likely to be so in a world that is ICT hungry, and low ICT penetration does not mean that the population is ICT hungry. The argument is more pertinent in case of ICT (because it is only a technology) and can also be used, among many, for narrower interest that may actually hinder economic and social development in_a wider sense. A holistic approach, in the present context, demands clarity of the phrases like 'remote' and 'rural' as socio-economic categories, and how we visualize the role of ICT in dealing with 'remoteness' and 'ruralness'. The problem becomes more evident when we try to elaborate 'demand' in Daly's conceptual framework. In his conceptual framework, demand and supply are responding to each other instantaneously. In fact, much of the problem of ICT for rural and remote areas is the lack of instantaneous responses between the two. ICT entails high capital cost, and demand for ICT services in rural and remote areas are governed by many factors that are outside the realm of ICT supplies. In other words, the model assumes the existence of a ready information market; and, therefore, assumes what it is supposed to create.

Context specific evaluation methodology

This approach suggests a context specific framework. It is argued that for different projects, having different social or economic goals to achieve, a generalized framework for evaluation might not be effective. Context specific evaluation helps to draw attention to the particular issues like health, education, etc. It is easier to monitor the impact for a particular issue. Some kind of generalization and the development of a common approach is possible by grouping the goals under a few main themes (O'Neil, 2001).

Distinctiveness of each project in terms of local interest, specific goals to be achieved, and objectives of the projects, necessitates the context specific evaluation. At the same time, by making context specificity as the critical aspect we tend to overlook the need for theoretical generalization for an evaluation framework. Specificity does not have any lower limit till we reach an individual as an analytical category. It is the overarching theoretical understanding that can legitimize the programme and its context specificity. However, the basic problem behind developing a standardized evaluation frameworks, and a set of indicators lies somewhere else. And that is the 'ICT centric' approach to the problem. What is it that makes ICT related projects context specific? Is it because they are located in different politico-socio-economic and environmental conditions? At a higher level of conceptualization, it is the nature and extent of use and non-use of information (and thereby use and non-use of ICT) that provides the context specificity and also the basis for comparison and comparable indicators.

Demand pull approach

Loosely stated, the approach proposes to build up ICT services, the appropriateness of which would be determined by the assessment of demand at the target community level. The Information Village in Villianur, Pondicherry, India, run by the M.S. Swaminathan Research Foundation (MSSRF) provides relevant information to the villagers through Information Shops located in the surrounding villages. The information need is assessed by using historical experiences of the other developmental projects and also by undertaking the base-line surveys. The ICT services are based on contents relevant to local needs. Villagers are provided information on weather, water, health, pest and disease management, marketing, etc. through information bulletins available in the Information Shop. The project addresses the question of immediate information needs of the community, and does not offer any direct access to technology to the villagers. An

ILO project at Warana Nagar rural network project (ILO, 2001) also aims at providing the need based information to the marginal communities without any direct access to technology.

The Duncombe and Heeks (2001) model integrates both access and needs. The model suggests the assessment of both ICT readiness and information needs of the target community to determine the appropriate technology level that the people would be comfortable to use for their benefits. They suggest that the ICT readiness capability building has to be part of the telecentre projects.

A Synthesis of Evaluation Methodologies

The theoretical contour suggested above is indicative of a transformation process. While it is quite close to the 'Whole System' approach as it does not suggest any linear relations between ICT and economic/social parameters, it also indicates the transformation process through informatization. Both information village project and the Duncombe-Heeks model are static in essence, because, like the Whole System approach, they also do not suggest the transformation process and, therefore, do not suggest indicators for impact evaluation. At the same time, both the approaches match the suggested theoretical contour in terms of the intervention needed at the initial stage of transformation. The issue of ICT readiness and the need for ICT capability building (Moyo, 1996) are essential ingredients of the transformation process. Both these approaches ignored the underlying importance of formal and informal education and enhancement of cognitive abilities as the key to rural transformation. This aspect has been ignored because none of these approaches actually stretched the process of intervention from the state of marginal economies to the status of developed economies.

Towards Workable Indicators

The understanding presented so far is helpful for identification of basic issues for indicators. We have argued that telecentres are for activating the transformation process of the marginal economies. There are three stages in the life of a telecentre project, namely, the initial stage, stage of transformation, and the post transformation. It is also argued that with the increased informatization there will emerge individual enterprises, and the economic activities would become more diversified and outwardly. This would be reflected in the diversification of the production and service activities along with the increased export and import from the region. Another characteristic change would be the transformation of the target community from information receiver to information seeker. That would be the beginning of the emergence of the information market. These end results would be achieved only when the transformation process has been adequately activated. We argue that ICT-based services have to be intertwined with other social and economic development programme. This can be achieved by relevant content development coupled with extensive awareness development programme. Relevance of the contents offered can be ascertained by the extent of development-related programmes covered, and their connectivity with developmental agencies. Awareness development programmes also have to be built around the same. The expected end results being known and the transformation process being in place, the question regarding the impact of ICT remains to be ascertained. This has to be captured by assessing the extent and type of use of the ICT services by the target population. Answers to the questions, like, who are using the ICT services? What are the services being used? Purpose of using different services, and identification of the factors behind non-use, are likely to bring out the contribution of telecentres in the social and economic development of the target economies.

The Present Study

The present study is based on community access projects in six countries, namely, Tanzania, Nicaragua, Honduras, Mali, Vietnam and Bhutan. These countries offer six different socio-politico-economic conditions. Thus, for Tanzania, MCTs are located in the refugee camps and aimed at serving the refugees. In Nicaragua, the MCT project aimed at carrying health services in remote areas, whereas in Honduras the MCTs were supposed to make ICT available to the poor and economically backward section of population of the country. Mali is a less developed economy with a widely dispersed population deprived of benefits of modern living. MCTs in Mali connect the rest of the world with remote hamlets. Vietnam's economy is on the fast forward path. Visible changes are taking place in Vietnam economy and society. The Government has taken proactive role, making ICT accessible to every nook and corner of the country. Bhutan has been a quiet Himalayan state even a decade back. Economic and social lives in villages of Bhutan are still very simple. Villages are located in distant and difficult terrain without any modern means of communication among them. ICT access programme in Bhutan makes use of the existing Postal network to provide access to the public and improve postal services.

A Cross-section Study of Economic Transformation

Any impact assessment study compares the pre-project scenarios with the post-project ones. The present study does not have this advantage, because no pre-project study has been carried out with a uniform framework. The countries for which MCTs were studied (as mentioned above) offer different phases in the whole range of the transformation process (marginal economy to economy on the fast track of development). The case of MCT in Mali is one of intervention in a marginal economy. Bhutan would be a shade better, because it has reasonably stable agricultural activities and increasing rate of literacy. The economy of Vietnam is developing very fast along with 100 % literacy among its younger population. Honduras, placed between Bhutan and Vietnam, is a case of high literacy rate with inadequate economic opportunities for its people, a large part of which migrate out for jobs. These four cases, therefore, offer a unique opportunity to observe the impact of the MCT project on the four stages in the process of transformation. The effort has been made to understand the factors that govern the ICT use pattern, and also the actions that would make MCT services more effective. The cases of MCTs in Tanzania and Nicaragua are treated separately. The Nicaraguan case actually is a case of enhancing the efficiency of health network system for providing services to rural and remote areas. Here, although the common citizens of rural and remote areas are the beneficiaries, they do not interact directly with ICT. For Tanzania it is a case of bringing ICT for the help of people in refugee camps, where neither a settled economy nor a society is in existence. When compared, the six cases presented here can be stated as follows. The four cases that refer to transformation process are the ones where government initiatives with international cooperation bring in ICTs for direct access by the citizens. The Tanzanian case also refers to the case of direct access to a group of people who are actually stateless. Therefore, the expected impact of ICT does not fall into the theoretical contour suggested above. On the other hand, in the Nicaraguan case, state's presence is predominant in providing health-related and disaster management-related services to its citizens.

The Questionnaire-based Survey

A questionnaire-based survey was conducted in the villages served by MCTs. Surveys were conducted with the help of the project staff. The questionnaire had three components.

The first component was to collect information mostly on the present status of the project in terms of services being provided, extent of use of the facilities by the local people, identification of the impediments in delivering the projected services, and also cost and revenue scenario. Most of this information was expected to be available from the local project authorities.

The second part of the questionnaire was for the project authorities to account for their assessment and experience about the outcome and management of the project, and suggestions on its sustainability and replicability.

The third part of the questionnaire was intended to identify and understand the factors that can discriminate between users and non-users of MCT facilities. The survey was designed to examine the social and economic discriminants between users and non-users of MCT facilities. Users and non-users were chosen from the villages benefited from the MCT services.

As expected, the questionnaire was not of much relevance for the cases in Tanzania and Nicaragua. While the third part of the questionnaire was mainly relevant for Tanzania, it was only the first two parts of the same questionnaire relevant for Nicaragua. The main limitation of the study is the lack of uniformity in the reports received from the country level experts. The report received from Bhutan is quite elaborate but could not follow the pattern suggested by the questionnaire. Difficulty in accessing the terrain, language barrier and social and economic situations made questionnaire-based investigation quite difficult there. The same was the problem with Mali and Tanzania. Although not in uniform format, information received from these countries has been used to create a comparable basis with other countries.

Country level studies are presented in four different chapters in the order: Mali, Bhutan, Honduras, and Vietnam

– from marginal economy to the economies on the development mode. These chapters are followed by the study of Nicaragua, a case of proactive state, and the case of Tanzania refugee camps—the case of stateless people, in two separate chapters.

Footnotes

1 The concept of limited cognitive ability, as defined by Simon (1957), had influenced the understanding of human behaviour and economic decision making, and established the importance of organization in subsequent economic ideas. In the present context the concept is used for distinguishing two individuals in an extended Simonian sense.

2 The argument, although does not directly follow, is developed from the reading of Leontev (1978, 1981).

3 This does not mean that the community breaks up at this point. It only indicates that, in terms of information, the community undergoes an evolution. It emerges as a socio-anthropological category, and gradually ceases to be a community as an economic category.

4 This section is extensively based on Jane Millar's unpublished report for ITU entitled 'Measurement of the Impact of Information and Communication Technologies (ICTs) in Rural and Remote Areas'.

2

MCT in Mali (Timbuctu)

The Case of a Marginal Economy

Present Status

The MCT in Mali is located in the desert town of Timbuctu, 1000 km from Bamako, the capital city. The MCT project has started its activities in October 1999.

For a period of three years the project had a budget of US$ 856 541, shared between International (US$ 423 550) and National partners (US $ 432 991) as per the details given in Table 2.1. After the end of the project period, in 2002, the MCT has been franchised to a private operator on a monthly rent of US$ 455.

Table 2.1: Funding of MCT (in US$)

Years	IDRC	ITU	UNESCO	FAO	WHO	Govt.	Mali Tel	Total
1999–00	77 000	69 850	61 000	18000	10000	212011	105460	553321
2000–01	15 000	13 850	53 500	0	30000	33000	24760	170110
2001–02	10 000	14 850	50 500	0	0	33000	24760	133110
Total	102000	98 550	165000	18000	40000	278011	154980	856541

The capacity of the local telephone exchange was found to be inadequate to meet the needs of the project. Later connectivity to the MCT was provided by a VSAT link using Intelsat satellite. In the early phase the inadequate capacity of the local telephone exchange and high-speed Internet connection between Bamako and Timbuctu affected the development of applications such as telemedicine.

Cost and Use of Services

Both capital and operational costs incurred during the project period are shown in Table 2.2.

Table 2.2: Cost incurred (in US$) over the project period (year-wise)

Years	Capital cost	Operational cost
2000	386901	60960
2001	85390	59960
2002	67150	65960
Total	539441	186880

As usual, capital cost was declining subsequently from the maximum in the first period. The operational cost was gradually increasing as new services were being extended over the project period.

Was there increasing incidence of accessing the services by the villagers around the MCT? Table 2.3 shows the use pattern of the services provided by the MCT. The table shows decline in the number of users and also the number of new users from the third year of the project.

Table 2.3: Use pattern of the services (year-wise)

Use pattern of different services	Service types					
	Telephone and fax (1 unit = 5mt)			Internet		
	2003	2004	2005	2003	2004	2005
Unit price (in US$)	0.23	0.23	0.23	1.8	1.8	1.8
Use in time units	24960u	24960u	22880u	9000h	9000h	9000h
No. of users	1200	1300	1100	6000	6000	5500
No. of new users	120	150	140	300	300	275

Socio-economic Profile of Villages

ICT penetration, when counted only in time unit, does not reflect the extent of the use of the ICT by the people of the marginal community. When read with the following other Tables on different socio-economic indicators and use pattern of ICT, it becomes clear that use of the MCT facilities is restricted only in the town of Timbuctu. Table 2.4 gives the profile of the villages studied for understanding the users and pattern of use of the services. Timbuctu is urban area, and the MCT is located in the town. Other villages studied are Kabara, Koreome, and Nibket AI Iik. These villages were chosen because users were mainly from these villages.

Table 2.4: Village profile

Village profile	Name of the villages			
	Kabara	Koreome	Nibket Al lik	Timbuctu
Distance from MCT	9 km	18 km	52 km	0
No. of household	37	40	9	1300
Total population	350	400	122	25000
Literacy (%)	18	12	5	60
General Economic Condition	Poor	Poor	Poor	Average

Distinctive features of the villages are their small size, poverty, large families and lack of literacy. The use of MCT is, therefore, restricted mainly to Timbuctu where MCT is located. It is evident from the Table 2.4 that the other villages are located too far from MCT, and also economically and socially too distant to become potential users of MCT services.

The typical economy of the villages is given in Table 2.5, which reflects the ruralness of the areas.

Table 2.5: Economy and the Ruralness

Name of theVillages	Sectoral contribution (%)				
	Agriculture	Minerals	H'hold Industry	SMEs	Other
Kabara	75	X	5	X	20
Koreome	80	X	10	X	10
Nebket Al lik	5	X	25	X	70
Timbuctu	70	X	15	X	15

The household industries are traditional rural handicrafts, and they are at dying stage. The column 'Other' includes occupations that are not regular, or only seasonal. Agricultural practices are completely traditional and productivity is very low.

The remoteness of the villages under study is shown in Table 2.6.

Table 2.6: Remoteness of the villages

Parameter	Name of the villages			
	Kabara	Koreome	Nibket Al lik	Timbuctu
Distance of the nearest market	0	0	52	0
Distance of the nearest hospital	9	18	52	0
Distance of the nearest higher education centre	9	18	52	0
Distance of the nearest post office	9	18	52	0

Timbuctu town has health, education and communication facilities. For rest of the villages Timbuctu is the nearest centre for modern amenities. Table 2.6, when read with Table 2.4 and 2.5, showing the villages around Timbuctu, gives us exact real cases of marginal economies described in the theoretical contour in Chapter I. These villages are poor in terms of physical infrastructure. As shown in Table 2.7, most of the villages do not have regular electricity or proper road network.

Table 2.7: Infrastructure in the villages

Infrastructure types	Name of the villages			
	Kabara	Koreome	Nibket Al lik	Timbuctu
Road network	Good	Good	Bad	good
Main modes of transport	Public/ own	Public/own	Public/own	Public/Own
Electrification	Partial	Partial	Rare	Full
Availability of electricity	Rare	Rare	Rare	Regular

The villages are the extreme examples of rural and remoteness. The ICT use pattern is likely to be governed by these socio-economic parameters, as depicted in Table 2.8.

Table 2.8 does not reflect the actual status of the ICT use in the villages other than Timbuctu. Use of ICT is not known much in these villages. For the villages having traditional economic activities and being too distant from modern economic practices, the extent of ICT readiness is not likely to be anything better than occasional.

Table 2.8: The pattern of ICT use in the villages

ICT services	Name of the villages			
	Kabara	Koreome	Nibket Al lik	Timbuctu
Postal service	Occasional	Occasional	Occasional	Occasional
Telephone	Occasional	Occasional	Occasional	Main
Telefax	Occasional	Occasional	Occasional	Occasional
Internet	Occasional	Occasional	Occasional	Main
Mobile	Rare	Occasional	Occasional	Main

Profile of the User and Non-user

Given this overall scenario, the questionnaire-based survey was to understand the users and non-users profile. Table 2.9 gives the survey details.

Table 2.9: Number of user and non-user of MCT services surveyed

Survey category	Villages surveyed			
	Kabara	Koreome	Nibket Al lik	Timbuctu
Users	7	8	5	10
Non-users	5	6	5	10

The main problem of any questionnaire-based survey of the villages around the MCT was difficult accessibility because of the remoteness and size of the villages, and resulted in a small number of respondents. An intuitive expectation was that use of ICT-based services would be strongly influenced by the livelihood pattern of the villagers. Table 2.10 gives some idea of livelihood of the users and non-users of the ICT services.

Table 2.10: Livelihood of the users and non-users

Villages	Main sources of income					
	Farming		Business		Service	
	User	Non-user	User	Non-user	User	Non-user
Kabara	5	3	2	2	0	1
Koreome	6	4	1	1	1	1
Nibket Al lik	4	4	1	1	0	0
Timbuctu	5	6	3	2	2	2

Activities like farming, business or service should be understood in the context of the general state of the economy of these villages. None of these activities are taken up for earning prosperity. These are the traditional family occupations, and families are continuing the same low income-generating activities, as nothing else is available. 'Business', therefore, means petty trading that hardly earns two meals a day. General economic status being the same across the occupation, profiles of the users and non-users of ICT are not likely to be any different.

We have taken population in the age group 15 to 40 as the potential ICT user. Is it that the user families have larger number of members in this age group? Table 2.11 provides information for the surveyed families.

Table 2.11: Number of family members in the ICT user age group (15–40 years)

Villages	Types	Families having number of family members in 15-40 age group				
		Two	Three	Four	Five	Six +
Kabara	User	0	2	4	0	1
	Non-user	2	1	1	0	1
Koreome	User	0	1	3	1	3
	Non-user	3	2	0	1	0
Nibket Al lik	User	0	0	1	1	3
	Non-user	3	1	1	0	0
Timbuctu	User	3	4	1	1	1
	Non-user	1	3	3	2	1

As we have seen earlier, family sizes in the villages are quite large, having, on an average, 10 members a family. Number of family members in the ICT age group (15–40) is also large. The large number in ICT age group does not lead to extensive use of ICT, because in a tradition-bound economy with very little alternative economic opportunities, the extent of ICT use is limited to emergencies only. Since literacy is positively related to ICT use, the survey also tried to examine if number of school going children or children in higher education in a family is a distinguishing factor between the user and non-user families. Tables 2.12 and 2.13 present information on that.

Table 2.12: Number of school going children in the families surveyed

Villages	Types	Families having number of school going children				
		Two	Three	Four	Five	Six and more
Kabara	User	0	0	3	2	2
	Non-user	1	2	1	1	0
Koreome	User	1	1	1	2	3
	Non-user	2	1	2	1	0
Nibket Al lik	User	0	2	2	0	1
	Non-user	2	2	1	0	0
Timbuctu	User	1	1	3	4	2
	Non-user	3	3	2	1	1

The social and economic status of the users and non-users being the same, the number of school going children does not make much distinction. It may be mentioned here that in Vietnam, the school going children are the major users of Internet. But, that is the story of a different economy which is undergoing rapid transformation.

Table 2.13: Number of families having children going for higher education

Villages	Types	Number of families having children going for higher education			
		One	Two	Three	Four or more
Kabara	User	1	1	0	0
	Non-user	1	0	0	0
Koreome	User	2	1	0	0
	Non-user	1	0	0	0
Nibket Al lik	User	0	0	0	0
	Non-user	1	0	0	0
Timbuctu	User	5	3	2	0
	Non-user	2	1	0	0

The village Nibket Al Iik, the poorest and remotest among the villages under study, has one family having one member going for higher education. This family is the non-user of ICT services. While exposure to higher education is expected to create demand for use of ICT, the poor economic condition restricts the use of the same in the present case.

Higher number of earning members, meaning higher income for the family, should be associated with higher use of ICT services. Table 2.14 explores this for the surveyed families.

Table 2.14: Number of earning members

Villages	Types	Number of families having number of earning members			
		One	Two	Three	Four or more
Kabara	User	1	4	1	1
	Non-user	0	1	1	3
Koreome	User	0	3	3	2
	Non-user	0	1	2	3
Nibket Al lik	User	0	2	1	2
	Non-user	0	1	3	2
Timbuctu	User	1	3	3	3
	Non-user	2	3	4	1

It is to be noted that most of the families have more than one earning member. This is an indicator of economic hardship of the families where, in many cases, even children have to work for bare necessities.

Table 2.15 gives the overall economic status of the both user and non-user families surveyed.

Table 2.15: Economic status of the families

Villages	Types	Income group		
		Higher	Middle	Lower
Kabara	User	0	4	3
	Non-user	0	1	4
Koreome	User	1	3	4
	Non-user	0	2	4
Nibket Al lik	User	0	1	4
	Non-user	0	1	4
Timbuctu	User	3	4	3
	Non-user	1	3	6

There are users and non-users in all income categories. No pattern is easily discernible. While the economic condition of the family is an important determinant of the use of ICT, the level and type of economic activities of the families and of the region also contribute to the ICT use pattern. Given the poor economic conditions of the villages and almost total absence of any modern economic activities, as well as social and economic amenities, the use of ICT is likely to be negligible irrespective of the relative economic status of the families.

Table 2.16 is about the awareness of the user and non-user families of the benefits from access to ICT.

Table 2.16: Awareness of the families about use of ICT

Villages	Types	Main mode of Communication	Main purpose of use of ICT	Perceived benefit	Suggestion
Kabara	User	1, 2	1, 2, 3, 4, 5	1, 2	1, 2, 3
	Non-user	1, 2	1, 2, 3, 4, 5	1, 2	1, 2, 3
Koreome	User	1, 2	1, 2, 3, 4, 5	1, 2	1, 2, 3
	Non-user	1, 2	1, 2, 3, 4, 5	1, 2	1, 2, 3
Nibket Al Iik	User	1, 2	1, 2, 3, 4, 5	1, 2	1, 2, 3
	Non-user	1, 2	1, 2, 3, 4, 5	1, 2	1, 2, 3
Timbuctu	User	1, 2	1, 2, 3, 4, 5	1, 2	1, 2, 3
	Non-user	1, 2	1, 2, 3, 4, 5	1, 2	1, 2, 3

Note: Entries mean that even if one respondent says that he uses ICT for business purposes, the response is entered as use of ICT for the village of the respondent.

Main mode: 1. Telephone; 2. Internet; 3. Fax; 4. Postal services

Main Purpose: 1. Social interaction; 2. Study/education; 3. Business; 4. Profession; 5. Career Health/Hygiene; 6. Market; 7. Security; 8. Any other

Perceived benefit: 1. Social interaction; 2. Study/education

Suggestion: 1. Lower the cost of accessing services; 2. Train people, and create awareness; 3. Better connectivity and speedier Internet connection.

The important points to be noted from the Table 2.16 are the following. The ICT readiness of the villages in the MCT areas is bare minimum, and restricted to telephone and Internet. The benefits perceived from ICTs are restricted to social interaction and education. Although there are respondents from users of ICT for business and other purposes, their number is too negligible to be counted. Over all, most of the villages and villagers actually are non-users of ICT for any purpose that would have any significant impact on the economic and social activities. From the suggestions of the respondents, it is clear that cost of the services is one of the deterrents, as is the lack of awareness.

Observations on the MCTs in Timbuctu

The MCT at Timbuctu is an example of creating access to extreme rural and remote areas in terms of all social and economic parameters. The MCT services here are targeted to individual needs, as it is in Honduras or Vietnam where social and economic conditions are much favourable to ICT acceptance in terms of literacy and diversity of economic activities. In the cases such as Timbuctu, a Nicaragua type MCT projects would generate more visible benefits. The 'information village' model, as experimented in India, will also have larger impact in creating demand for information and ICT services. As discussed in the chapter on the theoretical contour, a case of marginal economy has to have access to ICT services free of cost and services on assessed need for information are to be developed and provided to the communities.

3

E-Post and Telekiosks in Bhutan

A Marginal Economy in Transition

Telekiosk Project in Bhutan

The issue of connectivity and development in the context of Bhutan has been studied twice; once after the e-post project was launched, and again five years later when project was to be declared as completed. The Bhutan project was to initiate the unique idea of e-post through post offices to reach the remotest corners of the country in difficult Himalayan terrain. During the 2005 study we were blessed with the enthusiasm of the project team and the management of the Bhutan post regarding the promise of e-post for connectivity. By 2008, the situation had changed in interesting directions. Mobile telephony, which had been almost non-existent in Bhutan, swept away the efficacy of e-post. At the same time the e-post project that initiated Bhutanese society to the new age of connectivity through ICT was increasingly being embedded in the social and economic fabric of this previously quiet economy. Thus the case of Bhutan offers a unique opportunity and interesting insight to the issue of ICT for development.

Some important learning points are: (a) the initial enthusiasm with e-post was not misplaced; (b) initiation to ICTs is to be done through an appropriate programme; and (c) it is quite likely that, once initiated, ICTs will make their own inroads in many different ways depending on the pace and directions of the changes in the economy. E-post, nevertheless, remains an important means of initiating ICT to non-initiated remote and rural economics of Asia, Africa and Latin America. Keeping this fact in mind, the first part of this chapter presents the first phase of the e-post project in Bhutan. The second part of the chapter presents the main findings from the second phase, the full version of which is available as ITU document entitled, "Satellite Connectivity to Remote Areas and E-Services for Development: Initiatives through Post Office Telekiosks in Bhutan", ITU, Geneva 2009.

In simplest term the project aims to use new technology to quicken the communication between individuals and/or groups with the help of available and proven new technology. Bhutan offers the right case with its difficult terrain, inadequate communication system, particularly between remote areas and also between urban areas and remote hamlets in higher altitudes or across higher altitudes. The project proposal sets the sight to the future of a nation-wide digital infrastructure from which other digital services would flow, and would create a modern e-society.

As for the implementation plan, the scope of the project is narrowed down, first to address the 'written communication' segment through the establishment of Telekiosks in selected post offices. The already existing postal network of Bhutan Post has been taken as the launching pad and the main executing agency in Bhutan for this purpose. Since the backbone of the new technology is the telecommunication system, Bhutan Telecom was made a partner for the implementation of the project. Together, Bhutan Post and Bhutan Telecom selected thirty eight post offices that had reasonable postal infrastructure as well as stable telecommunication services. In addition, five remote post offices were also to be tele-linked by VSAT connection with technological and financial help from India.

From the information available with the Bhutan Post it has been seen that the normal postal delivery among these post offices, in some cases, may take as long as six days or more. Under normal conditions, according to Bhutan Post officials, delivery time in the remote post offices is about four days. It has been envisaged that through proper technological intervention the time could be brought down to two days or less. The mode of intervention has been planned through the establishment of Telekiosks that would connect those who have access to web technology with those who do not. Telekiosks would be equipped with an Internet connected computer system, a scanner and a printer. A letter either can be typed in the system, or a hand written letter can be scanned and then e-mailed to the nearest post office of the delivery point. At the receiving post office, the message would be printed and hand delivered to the addressee. The minimum achievable through this intervention would be shortening the inter-post office delivery time. More enduring benefit, however, would be familiarizing Bhutanese society with the digital communication system and unleashing the potential economic and social benefit that such technology could catalyse.

The proposal also foresees upstream and downstream connectivity of Telekiosks. All the post offices can be linked with the General Post Office at Thimpu, the capital of Bhutan, through servers for centralized data-base, more value-added services and data communication. Similarly, at the down stream, e-mailed messages can be down-loaded to a hand held system (Simputer, for example, is already being offered by an Indian firm) to be delivered at the end point. It is also envisaged that every household and even individuals can be given a unique e-address for e-post as well as e-mail communication. Individuals can use either the hand held portable system or the facility in any post office for e-mail/e-post services.

The implementation plan of the project consisted of three phases. A total of thirty eight locations have been chosen for establishing Telekiosks. These locations were chosen on the basis of available infrastructure, and revenue generation potentiality. Seventeen post offices were to be connected in the first year, followed by thirteen in the second year and eight in the third year. Subsequent phases would be taken up after evaluation of the first phase of the project and also on the basis of the responses from national and international agencies for mobilization of resources.

There are five extremely remote locations where access takes three to seven days on foot. These locations as such do not satisfy either the infrastructure or the revenue generation criterion, but offer a most challenging part of the project in terms of long-term social benefits to the people who are at present farthest from modern ICT.

Despatch schedule of a Bhutanese Post Office

Salient Highlights of the Project

The core value of the project is extending the benefit of ICT to those people of the country who are at the other side of digital divide—the ICT have-nots. The mainstay of the implementation plan is technology blending, i.e. the blending of modern means of communication with that of traditional (in case of Bhutan). The nature and extent of blending was determined by the compatibility of the new technology with the existing organizational infrastructure. The project has used the time-tested wide organizational network of delivery system of the Bhutan Post for carrying out the project. Steps for implementation are quite cautious, in fact, appear to be over cautious. So, as a first step, the project envisaged the introduction of new technology mainly to link selected Post Offices. The cautious initial steps are understandable, given the wide technological gap between the organizational demands of the new technology and the existing infrastructure. The steps appear to be over cautious because of uncertainty about revenue generation potential and the long-term sustainability of the initiative vis-à-vis the investment commitments from multiple sources. As we shall argue later, such an initiative needs to be justified more in terms of intangibles that it potentially generates in the form of social benefits, than in terms of monetary accounts in traditional balance sheet.

The project document refers to the feasibility study done by the Indian Institute of Management, Ahmedabad (IIM-A) as the background and justification of the project proposal. As for justification, the IIM-A study emphasizes the importance of social access to ICT over individual access. The original proposal recognized this and proposes a model with detailed logistics of technological and organizational aids to ensure social access to electronic communication, and hopes that the model would dispense "with the need for an individual to be literate, computer literate, well-off, and to have technological access". When it comes to the potential of telekiosks for revenue generation, the proposal recommended the pricing of new services not to exceed the minimum postal rate for an ordinary letter, as it exists at present. The proposal hoped that the Telekiosks would generate revenue from e-mail and e-post services. At the same time the proposal has been cautious to recognize that the idea being new in Bhutan much of the revenue generation would depend on its acceptance by the people of Bhutan and popularity of the services rendered. The question of sustainability (in terms of revenue generation) of such a project like this having target beneficiaries from a country like Bhutan is more complex.

Methodological Note

In the course of investigation for the present evaluation study, it has been perceived that evaluation methodology neither can be nor should be independent of the size and state of the recipient economy. As a methodological perspective, therefore, the present evaluation study uses revenue-cost calculations only for the last instance. The defence for this perspective is the fact that such ventures are not profitable on the basis of simple arithmetic calculations. Had there been any trace of profit from such ventures, the private initiatives would have grabbed it by this time. If there is any doubt about the entrepreneurial ability of Bhutanese, it is to be noted that there is no dearth of non-Bhutanese entrepreneur in Bhutan, who are known for their business acumen as well as penchants for new ventures. It is also to be understood that modern ICT-based services incur high initial costs, and that the general business practice across the globe is to go for volume to afford a lower price. Thimpu, the capital city of Bhutan, has a population of 30,000, the highest among all habitats in Bhutan. There are villages with only one household. Total estimated population of Bhutan is 0.65 million. Therefore a volume driven business model is ruled out for Bhutan. A price-driven business model, however, had never been feasible even in developed countries, and not applicable to the smallest and underdeveloped economies of the world.

Thus, the economic value of introducing ICT rests not only on the business of ICT itself, but also the way it can contribute to the enhancement of productivity in the Bhutanese production system. In an abstract sense, ICT enables quick exchange of information among the individuals, groups, offices, etc. Information, when exchanged gets value added; and it is the value-added information that becomes new knowledge. Since productivity is enhanced by the application of new knowledge, the ICT provides an important gateway to uplift an economy. The basic distinction between a developed and an underdeveloped economy can be described in terms of how ICT is embedded within the production system. In a developed economy it is so much part of the production system that a separate functional trajectory of ICT is hardly noticed. It is in this kind of state of development that ICT can generate revenue from services it would provide. On the contrary, in an economy like in Bhutan, where ICT is marginally or only ornamentally linked with the production system, a business model for ICT services is quite far fetched. Therefore, the much talked about digital divide is not only the numbers of haves and have-nots of ICT, but is also to be understood in terms of integration of ICT with the production system of the economy.

Integration of ICT with the production system is a process that happens through active initiatives. Such changes take place through the changes in the social dynamics. In fact, ICT first brings in changes in many social practices and behaviour and thereby in social dynamics. It is this initiative that, we feel, is the core of the project. Hence, the success of the project, from this perspective, is not the cost-revenue balance of the ICT itself, but the initiation of a process that catalyzes integration of ICT in Bhutanese economy and society. The benefit generated in this process is social goods and largely intangible that has a long gestation period before conversion to tangible benefits. A project of this nature, therefore, has to see beyond the phases of its implementation time frame. We strongly feel that evaluation of such projects also should be done in terms of its capability of creating enough intangible benefits. How do we account for intangibles? The question does not have any easy answer. For the present purpose we can take an easy rout that is, how extensive and intensive is the use of the facilities created by the project and which section of the population is making use of the facilities.

With this understanding, the specific information and data have been sought from the domestic partners of the project (Bhutan Post and Bhutan Telecom), post office personnel who manage the hardware and services at the post office level, some of the users of the new services, a few enterprises that deal with IT related services in Bhutan, and also a few available studies and reports that provide IT readiness of Bhutanese society. In many cases information gathered is interview based, and in some cases it is hard data.

An extensive questionnaire-based survey, as it was carried out for MCTs in Vietnam, could not be undertaken for Bhutan, mainly because of the logistic problems. In addition to the difficult terrain, most of the villages are too small (sometimes consisting of just one household).

Phase One

This report is about First Phase of the project. Although in the original proposal the action for the project began sometime in July 2002, the account of the implementing agency in Bhutan, (i.e. Bhutan Post,) shows that, at Bhutan level, the project time frame had been from June 2003 to January 2004. However, the logistics of the project have been quickly set up then onwards. The main action components at the first phase have been:

- Feasibility study and preparation.

- Delivery and installation of physical resources, namely, computer systems, UPS, printer and scanner in all the seventeen selected post offices.
- Training of the Bhutan Post staffs, mainly postmasters of the seventeen post offices.
- Activating the connectivity.
- Training or building awareness of the customers or the beneficiaries of the project (user group training).

The total project cost for the first phase had three components namely, capital cost, running cost, and training cost. It is to be noted that more than 80% of the total cost was earmarked for training, and more than 68% of the training budget (55.5% of the total budget) for training of the staff of the Bhutan Post.

By December 2003, the full package of the hardware was delivered and installed in seventeen selected post offices. Training of the staffs of Bhutan Post was arranged, with one session in India (at Saharanpur, Near Delhi) and another at Thimpu. This had been followed by on-site and on-the-job training of the staffs of the seventeen post offices where systems were installed. This was done mainly by the personnel of the Central office of Bhutan Post at Thimpu as and when required by the staffs at the post offices.

By January 2004 all the seventeen post offices were equipped with Internet connectivity through Druk Net, the Internet service provider arm of Bhutan Telecom. This did not face much of a problem since all the post offices were already equipped with telephone lines and fax systems were already in operation in these post offices. E-mail services were being offered by many of these post offices from October-November 2003. Post offices having school, college or/and other educational institutes around, and also those places popular as tourist destination, had encouraging initial responses for the use of e-mail services.

E-post service, as envisaged in the project proposal, was yet to be started. It appeared from the discussion with the postmasters that they were not fully conversant with the idea. In general, most of the post offices were slow starters, and had yet to take active steps to popularize either the e-mail or the e-post services.

Training of the customers or building awareness of the services had not been done. This was one of the most important components of the first phase of the project, particularly when the services are absolutely new for the users of the postal services. As a result the main users of e-mail services were restricted to college and school personnel, students, teachers and visitors to the research institutions.

It is to be noted here that the post offices having telephone connections have successfully operationalized the fax system for money transactions (Money Order) replacing the old system. The new technology has been successfully introduced and popularized by Bhutan Post. The staffs of the post offices have been exposed to new technology and its possible uses in postal services. During our visits to a few post offices that were covered under the first phase of the project we observed how efficiently the staffs at the post offices handled money transfer instructions through fax messages. According to the postmasters the arrangement of money transfer through fax has substantially reduced their workload. However, similar kind of excitement or confidence, was not visible for computer-based Internet services. Some sort of hesitation on the part of postmasters was evident. Most of the postmasters think that they are still not well conversed with the machine and need more rigorous training before making the system fully operational.

Effectiveness of Organization, Management and Impediments

Literally, the project objectives for the first phase have been partially achieved in the sense of delivering and installation of hardware, training of the postmasters in the operations of Internet and other associated use of computers and accessories, and establishing internet connectivity and offering e-mail services. While this is the logistic arrangement of the project, the essence of the project is to make progressive interventions in the modes of communication of the common people through the package of the new ICT. The main derivable benefits from the projects at the first phase are:

(i) Internal communications from GPOs down to CMOs, through POs and APOs initially through Internet, then gradually through intranet/LAN.

(ii) Initiation of e-post at least among the post offices that are connected at the first phase.

(iii) e-mail services for the e-mail ready market.

Out of the above three derivable benefits from the first phase of the project, the first and third ones have been initiated using the logistics that has been set up (installing hardware at the selected post offices) with notable success. The second derivable benefit, however, is the critical one and may need more commitment and innovative means to build up awareness and eagerness among the uninitiated users of traditional postal services. It has been seen from the experiences of the rural development projects in many developing and less developed countries that they involve quite complex social and cultural issues of local nature. The project team, in such cases, will need, in addition to the knowledge of computer and training on hardware, training on management and monitoring of projects that envisages introduction of new technology in rural areas.

To understand the management of the project and its associated problems we have to have a look at the Bhutan Post as a business model, and also at its organizational structure. Bhutan Post was corporatized in 1999. The transition from a government department to a business enterprise is not easy, since in its latter incarnation, Bhutan Post has to survive on the commercial viability of its main business. As a corporate entity, Bhutan Post has redefined its business – from postal service to service of delivering anything that is deliverable. This has widened its business propositions. In this difficult mountainous terrain it is the delivery as a service that comes as toughest. Over the last five years, after its corporatization, Bhutan Post is still depending mainly on the traditional postal services, although it has tried to get into services like delivery of school books and stationery, and regular transport services to major urban centres in Bhutan and to Kolkata, India, with modest success. They are trying new business opportunities, because revenues from the traditional sources are showing a downward trend over last few years.

According to the postmasters, telephone services provided by the post offices are the singular most important reasons for the declining trend in the traditional postal services. Tele-density of Bhutan being very low and household subscription of telephones being rare, telephone facilities at post offices are widely used by the people for faster, cheaper and sure means of non-written communications.

Postal services in Bhutan have a four-tier structure. Bhutan is divided into four postal regions, namely, Thimpu region, Phuentsholling region, Gelephu region, and Samdrupjongkhar region. At the first tier, there are two GPOs (General Post Office)—one at Thimpu and another at Phuentsholling. There are twenty seven Post Offices (PO), ten Agency Post Offices (APOs), and seventy Community Mail Offices (CMOs). The POs are part of the regular postal services staffed by full time postal employees, whereas APOs are run by postal agents, mainly by retired or ex-postal employees for a fixed monthly allowance. Postal services are extended deep down to the village level through CMOs, and manned by the local government employees, schoolteachers, or a literate person in the village. The CMOs sell stamps and accept letters to be delivered either to the APOs or POs. A region-wise account of revenue generation shows that most of the postal districts have negligible access to the postal services. The Thimpu region has one GPO, five POs, three APOs, and 17 CMOs. There is hardly any postal communication between CMOs. Thimpu region includes the capital city and near-by comparatively prosperous town (including the only airport of the country). The POs in these places have better business. The rest of the APOs and CMOs do not generate any notable revenue. The picture is the same for Phuentsholling region that has one GPO, two POs, five APOs and thirteen CMOs. Gelephu region has six POs, two APOs, and seventeen CMOs. Samdrupjongkhar region has six POs, seven APOs, and twenty CMOs. If CMOs are said to be located at the hinterlands, then postal activities in Bhutan can be described as mainly between hinterlands and towns, between towns, and almost non-existent between hinterlands.

It appears from the above description that the future revenue generation potential of Bhutan Post depends much on its ability to extend postal communication among towns of different postal regions and also among CMOs. It is from this perspective that the present project offers an important intervention in the communication revolution of Bhutan. At the same time, establishing such communication networks across the country has significant cost and management implications, particularly because such an effort may not generate profit at the beginning and would entail a high gestation period. As a corporate entity, where performance is judged on the basis of profitability, Bhutan Post might not find such a venture attractive enough, until and unless it has substantial and assured financial and management support from external sources during the gestation period.

Telecommunication Network and Suitability of the Project

Bhutan Telecom, the only telecom service provider in Bhutan, is one of the domestic partners of the project. Druk Net, the sole Internet service provider is a subsidiary of Bhutan Telecom. Except for remote post offices, others have been already connected with telecom network. A few of the post offices that are not yet connected with telecom services and are parts of the selected post offices for the project, are to be taken up only at the third phase of the project through VSAT connection. All the seventeen post offices in the first phase of the project have already had telephone connections. These post offices, as mentioned earlier, are using fax systems for money transfers. Hence, providing Internet connection to these post offices has been achieved without any problem. Demand for Internet connectivity in Bhutan is very low, and concentrated only in two districts, Thimpu (80% of Internet connection), the capital city and Phuentsholling (10%), bordering with India, which have comparatively more vibrant business activities, more with India than with other parts of Bhutan.

There are two aspects of the low demand for Internet. First, at the present level of demand, there is not much load on the server of the Druk Net and the dial-up connection is reasonably fast for the use by post offices that are connected in the first phase of the project. Secondly, it is the impact on price of the Internet services due to low volume of demand. With around 1500 connections across the country the present price for every minute of Internet access is not cheap. Post offices under the project have been offered a package of 15 hours for Nu 850. Per minute Internet access cost at this rate becomes Nu 0.95. The rate is high enough to deter popular use of Internet in Bhutan.

For e-post, however, even the present rate could be economical if used judiciously. As we have mentioned earlier the load on the Internet service provider not being high, data transfer is reasonably fast. As proposed in the project document, if the e-post is made functional through scanner and printer, it is possible to send mail as attachment through Internet. Sending the attachment file should not take more than five minutes at the present speed of data transfer. Cost for five minutes of Internet use, at the present rate, would be Nu 4.75, which is less than the lowest postal charges in Bhutan. Economic viability of the proposed e-post at this stage would, therefore, depend upon the judicious use of computer, accessories and Internet. The postmasters have to take lead in this regard.

The present use of the facilities created by the project is restricted to e-mail services by individuals who are already in the fold of the world that is Internet savvy. It is e-post that would truly address the issue of digital divide by making the benefit of ICT accessible, directly or indirectly, to the society in general. Present telecom system is competent enough to cater to the present low level of demand, and it would remain so for some time to come because of slow growth of demand for telecom-based services. It is also for the interest of Bhutan Telecom and Druk Net to see that the project achieves success, because it is one of the sure ways to extend the use of Internet in Bhutan. At present both, Bhutan Telecom and Druk Net, are passive service provider. Both the organizations should actively promote the project objectives; take initiative for awareness development about the role that ICT can play in the social and economic life of Bhutanese. As already mentioned, although the building of awareness has been part of the project task, it has not been taken up at all. The implementation of the other parts of the project has been easier if kept restricted to procurement and delivery of the hardware systems in the selected post offices.

Attractive Bhutanese architecture

The Department of Information Technology, the organization that was supposed to take up the task of awareness building should have collaborated closely with Druk Net and Bhutan Telecom. This is a win-win proposition for all the partners, because in the process of taking up actions for building awareness regarding the use of ICT among Bhutanese communities, these organizations are actually enhancing their business volumes and opportunities.

Utilization of Facilities

Facilities that have been installed in each of the seventeen selected post offices are a computer system, an ink jet printer and a scanner. As mentioned in the earlier sections at present the facilities are mainly used for e-mail purposes. The service is functional in all the seventeen post offices. However, commercial service has been successfully initiated only in a few post offices. Six post offices have maintained very systematic information on the use of Internet time. First Internet connectivity was installed at Ranjung post office on 25 October 2003. The post office has maintained very detailed account of minute-wise Internet use. It has renewed its connectivity once till February 2004. For the first package, it's earning was Nu.1080 for a 15 hour package at Nu.850. In the second package, earning was Nu. 1230. Apart from the commercial use, Internet time has also been used for inter-post office communication on transaction issues like confirmation and clarifications of money orders received or/ and sent. Post offices that have educational institutes or research institutes around it enjoyed the privilege of e-mail ready market from among the students and faculties. Wangdue is one such post office. It has two very important research institutes, namely, Renewable Natural Resource Research Centre (RNRRC), and Natural Resource Training Institute (NRTI) with substantial international contacts located here. Students and faculty of these Institutes, many of whom are foreigners, are regular users of e-mail services at the Wangdue post office. Wangdue also attracts a lot of tourists, and hence foreign customers. Wagdue post office received Internet connection on 5 November 2004. From 7th November onwards it started getting customers. Till March 2004, Wangdue post office renewed its connection once. During this period its cost for Internet connectivity was Nu. 1700, and revenue earned was Nu. 2020. The rest of the Internet time has been used for communication with GPO at Thimpu, and also for testing and learning. Installed a few weeks later, Punakha post office also is quite privileged as a tourist destination as well as the presence of a higher educational institution. Punakha post office also has earned substantial revenue from e-mail services. However, it shows longer time for learning and testing and communication with GPO at Thimpu. These three post offices have kept most detailed account of Internet time use. Paro post office is an exception to the trend set by these three post offices. Although this post office serves a major town (with an airport) in the country, and also is a major tourist destination, the commercial success of Internet services of Paro post office has not been as easy as it has been in other three cases. From a comparison of the commercial use of the facilities in these four post offices, it appears that more than the transit tourists population (as in the case of Paro), existence of more permanent users like higher educational and research institutions explains the demand of e-mail services. The Paro post office did not renew its connection and did not maintain any account of Internet use. Trashigang post office has detailed record of the Internet use, but it did not renew the connection after the first package from which it earned Nu. 425 over about 20 days since inception on 1 December 2003. Mongar post office, on the other hand, has detailed data on minute-wise use for three months beginning November 2003, but neither gives information on type of use nor on the revenue earned. Samdrupjongkhar and Gelepu could make limited use of Internet connectivity because of recent disturbance of political nature in the areas of these two post offices. Available records of the use and discussion with postmasters confirmed the belief that much of the extensity of the use of the facilities depends on the interest and proactive initiatives of the postmasters. During discussion many postmasters have drawn attention to the small but important issues related to the facilities that are needed for effective functioning of Telekiosks.

Two such issues are: (i) space for the kiosks at the post office, and (ii) timing of the services. At present there is neither any dedicated furniture nor space for the computer and other accessories that are installed at the post offices. They are presently operated from the desk of the postmasters. This creates inconvenience to both the regular postal services and the new Internet services. The project should allow separate provision of furniture and space for the Telekiosks. Again the normal post office hour being 10 am–5 pm, Internet service cannot be provided after office hour; whereas demand for Internet services is mostly after 5 pm, when users have free time after their own working hours. This problem does not have any easy solution, because post offices cannot invest anymore for extended office hours.

Space is major problem for Telekiosks in Post Offices

Some of the other glitches have been taken care of by the Bhutan Post at the right time. One such has been the printer as part of the total hardware package of the project. The ink-jet type printer has been found unsuitable for operation at the field for various reasons. The running cost of ink-jet printers is quite high compared to the dot matrix printers. Also the ink that is used for such printers dries up if unused for some time. Given the low level of initial use of the printers, ink drying up has been a problem. Bhutan Post took the right decision of replacing all the inkjet printers with dot matrix types. Project staffs at Thimpu post office also suggest that instead of going for locally assembled computer, branded products would have been better in terms of reliability and services. However, given the small size of the computer market in Bhutan, and also taking into account the difficult hilly terrain away from Thimpu, it is doubtful if established companies would be able to deliver the services that could not be delivered by the locals.

The project management also has to look into the operational issues for smooth running of the project. Pricing of the Internet time use by the customer is to be streamlined and uniform over all the post offices. A uniform automated billing system has to be introduced as soon as possible. This will lend reliability to the system.

Presently Internet connectivity is subscribed by the 15 hours, Nu. 850 package. Project management should communicate its appropriate instructions to the post offices for renewal of the subsequent connectivity and source of fund for renewal, so that continuity in connectivity is ensured. This is more important for post offices that are yet to generate enough revenue to fund subsequent renewal.

The big question arises here about the running cost of the project. As we have indicated earlier, in addition to the running cost, the smooth functioning of the facilities would need additional infrastructural cost for furniture and space. Also to be sorted out is the problem of timing of the services of the Telekiosk beyond normal post office hours. All these can be ensured by ensuring the required flow of funds. While infrastructure related costs could be a part of the project budget in the subsequent phases, ensuring the flow of fund for running and maintenance costs remains an important issue. Is Bhutan Post in a position to bear the cost of running the facility over the gestation period? If not, the same should be a part of the project budget under separate budget headings.

The Sustainability Question

At the present initial level of the progress of the project, the facilities are being used practically by the e-mail ready market. As expected, the response has been quite brisk in some post offices, while it has been quite lukewarm in some other post offices. More extensive use of the facilities is expected once e-post services are introduced. In either of the cases the integration of ICT in the economic and social life of Bhutan will depend upon the proactive strategies of the post offices.

As for the sustainability of the project, it is clear from the above account of the use of the facilities that some of the post offices have shown positive balance between revenue and cost by providing e-mail services only. Over the period many other post offices may also return the similar result. Is that enough to call the project successful and sustainable? Answer is negative for two reasons. First, sustainability this way does not address the question of digital divide. In fact, it only widens the divide, because, as we have narrated earlier, the e-mail service at present caters to the e-mail ready market and does not take ICT to the have-nots. It is through e-post that the project envisaged to reach out to the larger section of the Bhutanese society. The first question that should be asked for measuring the success of the project is; how extensive the ICT use has become? It is not the sustainability in terms of balance sheet figures; it is maximization of social benefits from Telekiosks that has to be monitored. In the process, if enough revenue is generated to balance out the cost, that would be a dream-run for the project. However, such a scenario is unlikely in near future. There is no ready market for e-post, as is the case for e-mail. Not only the market, acceptance of e-post has to be created by active participation of the post offices and innovative programmes from the partners.

Can such programmes be implemented through private participation? Many officials in Bhutan Post and Bhutan Telecom are positive about it, although they are not very clear about the mechanism of coupling such partnership. A few points regarding private participation requires to be made clear at this stage. It is not true that whatever is not commercially profitable under public management would be turned around by the perceived efficiency of the private initiative. A project such as the present one is not profitable right now, not because it lacks private initiatives, but because its objectives are to generate social benefits that private initiatives would generally ignore. In other words, e-post or e-mail services have not come up in Bhutan under private initiatives only because they are not profitable at this moment. As we have seen previously, e-mail services alone have been able to recover just the running cost in a few post offices only. The minimum wage in Bhutan is Nu.100 per day. Any private venture to be attractive has to have a minimum return more than the minimum wage. If the existing level of Internet use is any indication, Telekiosks do not seem to be attractive for private venture still for some time to come.

Therefore the followup task should be concentrated on two aspects: First one is the maximization of the derivable benefits from the Telekiosks. These are extensive and intensive inter-post office communications, up and down the level of hierarchy. Second one is the popularization of e-mail use. This service has the potentiality to earn revenue for recovering the running cost. Last, but most important is the introduction of e-post. Together these three would ensure creation of wider base of ICT awareness and various possibilities of its use in the social and economic life of Bhutan. Once the base becomes wide, and ICT awareness increases, the use will increase and ICT will become a commercial business on its own right without aid from any external agencies.

Future Course of Action

Awareness and training of the beneficiaries

This is of utmost importance and has not been tried in the

first phase. It has been argued above that computer training of the postmasters has been over-emphasized. It is our firm understanding that instead of computer training, post office personnel should actually be given training on the needs of a proactive approach, and made part of the awareness-building programme.

Action in this regard should be spearheaded by the Department of Information Technology (DIT) in close collaboration with Bhutan Telecom (BT) and Bhutan Post (BP) and later through involvement of POs, CMOs and APOs. An apex body comprising BP, BT and DIT has to prepare an action plan for awareness- building programme and also a monitoring mechanism. The apex body could consider bringing in a private agency for executing such programme. The TV and Radio transmission networks may be effectively used for wide publicity of the gains from the initiatives.

However, on-field hands-on demonstration of the functioning of the programme, is the best way to build up the acceptance of the uninitiated common people. Demonstrators may carry hand-held equipment and can actually demonstrate the efficacy of the programme.

Trial run of e-post

It should be initiated immediately. The POs have to be ready with services along with the launch of an awareness building programme. The best way to begin with is to use the post office personnel themselves to communicate through e-post. Besides, a weekly inte-rpost office communication routine can be introduced to test-run the e-post and also to train post office people in e-post, so that they can effectively take part in the awareness-building programme.

The initial review of the project recommended that Bhutan Post should introduce an e-post practice regime for POs that have been covered in the first phase and to incorporate other POs as soon as they are equipped. For execution and monitoring of the e-post practice, a dedicated project team needed to be constituted at Bhutan Post.

Training of the dedicated project team in management and monitoring of the rural development project

Once the awareness building programme is taken up and e-post service is introduced, full time service of a project team for drawing up a work plan with a time frame and also for monitoring and reviewing of the progress as well as constraints encountered, would be essential. The project team also has to collect and collate information from POs on the extent and nature of uses of the facilities for monitoring the spread of digital access in the Bhutanese society. This has to be done at the Bhutan Post level. The monitoring of the progress in terms of intangibles, as argued earlier would need external inputs. Bhutan Post may consider regular reporting to the apex body for assessing the extensity and intensity of uses of facilities by the people.

Members of the project team may need appropriate knowledge on the critical aspects of project management and monitoring, particularly for the kind of projects that aims at introducing new technology into the social life of the rural economy.

Creation of provision for separate space and furniture

This lesson from the execution of the first phase should not be taken lightly. A visit to any of the POs covered under the first phase of the project would reveal how crucial the issue is. Also has to be thought of the arrangements for running the kiosks beyond the normal post office hours. This is very important from the revenue generation point of view. In fact, once e-post service becomes functional, POs may find it difficult to provide e-mail services during normal post office hours. We propose some sort of experiment with committed volunteers to provide services at least for a few hours beyond the normal post office hours. Particularly for POs having educational institutions around, this can be tried. The volunteers may be given a token of free Internet time.

Measures for keeping regular account

Bhutan Post being the executing agency for the project, it needed to issue appropriate instructions to the POs in this regard. It has been already discussed that Bhutan Post, as a corporate body, may not be in adequate financial position to bear the expenses of running cost for anticipated long gestation period (about 5 years) of the project. Therefore, there has to be an appropriate subsidy scheme for the running cost of the project. The ITU, UPU, and domestic partners (BP, BT, DIT) together have to evolve the scheme. Ideally, running the project through the gestation period should be integral part of the project budget.

Findings from the Study of Villages Served by MCTs in Bhutan

The following villages were studied.

- Chang Dunkar (Paro Post office),
- Jumthang (Punakha Post office),
- Kilkhorthang (Wangdue Post office),
- Laimai goenpa (Bumthang Post office),
- Chhuzagang (Gelephu Post office),
- Riotola (Zhemgang Post office),
- Bangtsho (Deothang Post office),
- Kilikhar (Mongar Post office),
- Samkhar goenpa (Trashigang Post office), and
- Buna (Rangjung Post office),

Taking into account the time constraints and the demanding logistics of surveying a low density settlements separated by rugged terrain, it was planned to cover only 60 users respondents and an equal number of non-user respondents.

Factors affecting access to ICT

It has been observed from the survey of the villages that users of ICT have household income above the poverty line. On the other hand, 72% of the non-users are also above the poverty line. It has also been seen that families above the poverty level are also the most literate families. Lack of diversified economic activities and enterprise appear to be determining factors behind ICT use.

Affordability

Another factor limiting the usage of ICT is the high cost of accessing the services. At the Telekiosks, currently, charges are Nu.2.50 per minute. This makes regular use of ICT beyond the reach of even the families above the average income level. Unfortunate fact is that Bhutan Telecom, which is the main provider of telecommunication services, does not give sale commission on ICT service provided through the telekiosks or MCTs. Consequently, the Telekiosks have no option but to add 10% to 15% above the connectivity charges levied by Bhutan Telecom. Thus, the only way forward to increase the customer base of the Telekiosks is to reduce the price of connectivity. This means the regulatory environment in Bhutan must be shaped to allow for communication technology to reach its widest audience cheaply.

Awareness of the ICT services is very poor among the villagers. While all the respondents knew about telephones, only 82% had seen a computer and none of them had actually used Internet or e-mail. In fact, most of the non-user respondents did not have an opportunity to use even a telephone. Given the fact that teledensity is only 1% in rural

Bhutan, access to technology is an impediment to the spread of ICTs. Recognizing the above, Bhutan was working towards ambitious targets in the extension of its ICT infrastructure before the end of the 9th Plan in 2007. Bhutan Telecom was engaged in an aggressive plan to roll-out at least 10 telephone lines to every Gewog by the end of the Five Year Plan in 2007, using Cor DEC and WiFi technologies. Additionally, DIT planned to pilot 70 MCTs in rural communities by 2007.

Although sufficiently disaggregated data on revenue generated from the Telekiosks are not readily available, it is known that, at the present level of functioning Telekiosks are unprofitable. This means investment on the Telekiosks can only be fully justified on the basis of social return. Social returns can be maximized by making Telekiosks services more diversified. One way of earning more revenue could be taking advantage of the following: (a) Telekiosks being a part of postal network, which by far is the most extensive network in the country; (b) available technology makes it possible to set-up such counter at a reasonable costs; and (c) optimum utilization of the Telekiosks to bring about wide range of services to the people.

In addition to the efforts to generate more revenue, Telekiosks also have to develop content and applications that are locally relevant. Discussion with villagers identified the following areas where information services could be useful to them.

Agriculture & Farming

- Market price of various agricultural produce.
- Management of cash crops.
- Procurement of grain grinders.
- Procurement of potato seeds.
- Mithun bull for insemination.
- Rural credit procedures.

- Timber extraction process
- Pesticide management in orange.
- Construction prohibition in wetland.
- SaThram transfer process.
- Payment for excess land.
- New farming technology options.
- BAFRA regulations.

Governance

- Draft Constitution.
- Decentralization (people's roles).

Development Plan & Finance

- Changes in development plans and budget allocation.
- Income tax procedures.

Law Enforcement

- Laws and legal procedures.
- Security clearance procedures.

Environment

- Environment conservation.
- Conservation of black-necked Cranes.

Registration

- Registration and census process.

Banking

- Banking and saving procedures.

Health

- More about HIV/AIDS.

Education

- Education options for Class X failures.

Transport

- Checkpost checking procedures for all types of vehicles.

ICT

- Awareness and usage.

Observations

The Bhutanese economy is predominantly agriculture based. The practice of agriculture is traditional. At the same time the agriculture is quite diversified, producing varities of fruits and vegetables other than the staple food crop rice. Although slow, the economy is gradually entering into non-agricultural activities, mainly in fruit processing industries and has made a mark in the export market of the neighbouring countries. Hydropower is one of the natural resources the country is blessed with, and, currently, it is constructing power plants for energy exports to the neighbouring countries. It is in this regard of economic opportunities that Bhutan is ahead of Mali. It is also different from Mali in terms of literacy. The universal literacy programme has created an educated younger generation who can easily take the advantage of ICT for creation of new enterprises.

The study finds that the telekiosk project, as it has been proposed, has great potentiality to address the issue of the digital divide in favour of the ICT have-nots. The study takes the perspective that such an initiative should anticipate a longer gestation period for the realization of full benefits. As already discussed, it is the high cost of accessing ICT services and the low income of the families that bottlenecks the ICT use. The MCT project, therefore, has to have a life extended till the ICT use synchronizes with economic activity. As observed earlier, what is needed is the increased efficiency of the project team for the development of relevant content, and building ICT awareness among the people. Bhutan as a whole offers the most potential case for transformation.

The Project Revisited in 2008*

Briefly described, the project has brought computerization in Bhutan Post. The impact is two-fold. The first one is internal to Bhutan Post in the form of changes in work culture, commitment, innovative initiatives, etc. and also in the form of demand for more computer-based services in the post offices. The other one is the Telekiosks-based services being provided to the communities in and around the post offices. The extent of use by the communities can be assessed from the revenue earned by post offices from these services. As we have seen, most of the revenue is actually generated from voice communication and Fax-based services. Use of Internet is at its infancy. While revenue earned is reasonable for some of the post offices, for many others it is yet to reach a significant level. Wherever there is growing demand for ICT-based services, emerging private enterprises take away share of the market. Post offices with higher organizational cost find it difficult to match the services provided by the private enterprises. Two factors limiting the use by communities are: (a) difficult terrain over which villages are spread makes such facilities unreachable for many villages, (b) the economic activities in Bhutan is not vibrant enough to generate increasing demand for ICT-based services. The study has brought out the fact that the facilities created by the project are actually being accessed by the villagers from very remote places. The value of this accessibility is to be understood from the relations between ICT access and economic changes in Bhutanese context. The

* The following section is adapted from the report, ITU-UPU, Satellite connectivity to Remote Areas and E-services for development: Initiatives through post office Telekiosks in Bhutan, ITU, Geneva, 2009.

statistical result of the macro level exercise relating to ICT and economic changes in Bhutan has shown that ICT contributes to the creation of economic diversity. And the increasing economic diversity enhances the use of ICT-based services. Seeing from this perspective, the inroad the project has made in the remote villages of Bhutan is more enduring than it is reflected by the data on revenue earned by the post offices.

Road blocks

As it happens always in such cases, the project faces quite a few road blocks. The ICT services through Telekiosks are giving reasonably good business to the post offices that are located closer to urban areas or having educational institutions around. In many cases private enterprises have come up and they are providing similar services at a lesser price. Post offices, due to higher organizational costs, find it difficult to compete with private service provider.

Whereever there is higher demand, there is also demand for faster connectivity. These post offices strongly feel the need for broad-band connectivity.

Issues

The road blocks are external to the project, and in many cases they are not foreseeable. Such situations require rethinking and revamping the cost, price and modes of services. There are issues that are internal to the system and the project. In the case of this project, the most important issues are the maintenance, repairing and replacement of the equipments. The problem has to be addressed keeping in mind the facts that once computerized, any break-down for a few days will cause collapse of the system. At present the problem is addressed on ad-hoc basis. There has to be planned resource mobilization for this purpose.

Challenges

The major challenge of the project is to ensure the sustainability of the Telekiosks. There is no short cut method of either reducing the cost or generating revenue to strike a balance between cost and revenue of the kiosks. This is more so for VSAT connectivity, where project cost is far higher than other kiosks. As we have stated at the outset, the project has achieved the goal of reaching the unreached. In this case, it was essentially through creating ICT infrastructure in post offices of Bhutan. The initiation to a new era of computerization has thrown new challenges to Bhutan Post. The future challenge remains in taking the ICT to the communities. Our considered view is that riding on the experiences of the project, and also from the experiences of the similar projects in Vietnam, the Telekiosks project can now be shifted to the local communities. What we are proposing is a business model with public-citizen partnership. The day to day management of the kiosk can be left with the representative of the local community after initial training of the reasonably educated community members. In case of Vietnam, the local communities employ their own personnel for managing the kiosk. S(he) is also paid by the local community as a percentage of the total revenue earned. The maintenance, repair and training are taken care of by the post office. A similar model can be considered for taking ICT to the community level in Bhutan. The mainstay of this proposal is not earning of more revenue, but to make ICT accessible and familiar to the local communities; and make them partner of the benefits as well as the cost of the services. This also lessens the burden of the post offices from the operation of the Telekiosks. The core of this proposal is the finding from the statistical exercise, which tells us that ICT contributes to economic changes. Carrying ICT to deep into the remote areas will have higher gestation period for break-even, but will lower the gestation period for economic changes, and, in turn, will create more demand for and revenue from ICT services .

If we rule out the option of no connectivity, the strategy is to mobilize resources, both from internal as well as external sources for funding the deficits. Our survey results show that in most of the Telekiosks, including the remote VSAT stations, revenue is increasing. It is not increasing at a pace that would quickly wipe out the deficits. Also, voice communication and fax services being main usage, there is not much diversification in the usage of the services. Our study on the economic dynamics of the ICT use in Bhutan show that extensive use is actually dependent on the extent of diversification of the economic activities, extent of education and state of physical infrastructure. The result is quite indicative of the fact that extensive use of ICT-based services of the Telekiosks will come along the way of creation of economic opportunities in Bhutan.

The Bhutanese economy shows many changes in the desirable directions. If employment pattern is any indication, it shows that after agriculture, construction sector is the most important employer. This indicates that physical infrastructure is on the path of development. Literacy has been always a positive aspect of Bhutanese developmental pathways. It has to be complemented with more opportunities for higher skill-oriented educational activities as well as opportunities for skill-based economic activities. As we know, extensive use of ICT is both cause and effect of the process of economic development. From the sustainability point of view, the required resources from internal sources can be mobilized only through the diversified economic activities of the country. As the economy grows, mobilization of resources become easier, and need for support from external resources become lesser. In fact, as the economy grows, demand for ICT services also grows and gradually reaches the volume for break-even.

However, none of these happen quickly, and never overnight. The big question, therefore, is how to sustain the Telekiosks till the demand for services reaches the required volume? The question is more important for Telekiosks in the VSAT locations, where even the maintenance of the stations incur very high cost compared to those having normal connectivity. Our understanding of the users, usage and the dynamics of the Bhutanese economy suggests the following:

1. At present kiosks are managed by post offices. Installations of the facilities are funded mainly from external resources. The beneficiaries are not aware of the cost-revenue aspect of the problem.
2. We expect that economic growth will create opportunities and employment for villagers. This is where resources will be generated through economic growth. We also expect that the process will generate more demand for ICT-based services in villages.
3. Involvement of the community/villagers in the management of the Telekiosks appears to be the desirable direction of changes in the management of the kiosks. This will relieve the post offices from the day-to-day management of the kiosks and relieve the post offices from the problem of shortage of manpower, a problem highlighted by all the post offices that participated in the survey.
4. The location of the kiosks requires to be shifted to a place to be allocated by the beneficiary community. This will save the space in the post offices occupied by the equipments meant for the kiosks. Because of the space problem most of the post offices find immense problem providing personal access to the computer to the prospective users of the services, like Internet access. Post offices also find problems providing services beyond the normal working hours

of the post office. This problem also can be resolved if the kiosks are managed by the beneficiary communities.

5. The beneficiary community will employ its own person to manage the day-to-day function of the kiosk. The employee, selected by the community, will have adequate knowledge and also will be trained by the post office personnel for the operations of various ICT-based services.
6. The employee thus selected and trained will impart training to the villagers on various computer-related usages on the basis of fees decided by the community.
7. Revenue earned from the access services and also from training of the villagers will go to the community, who will pay the employee a negotiated amount on monthly basis.
8. We visualize multiple benefits from the proposed change in management. Villager-users will be made aware of the cost-revenue issues of running the kiosk. It will also help spreading the computer and ICT deep down the community. Over and above, the expected economic growth will be immediately reflected in the demand for services, earnings from the kiosks, prices of the services etc. based on which the community will take decisions on nature, type, and prices of the services.
9. We visualize the role of post office mainly as overseeing the installation of the kiosks in the villages, training of the personnel, maintenance of the equipment, and also advising on the nature and types of new services, equipment, costs etc.
10. The process of shifting the kiosks to the communities has to be gradual. It has to begin with the kiosk having villages with reasonable number of users, persons with

adequate ability to bear the responsibility of managing the kiosk and also a community that is willing to take the responsibility. As such the VSAT-connected kiosks are going to be at the end of the process of shifting of management of the kiosks. This is not only because they are economically behind many others, the user villages are also dispersed and sparsely populated.

11. The resource that is needed for survival of the kiosks during the gestation period in between, has to be arranged by mobilizing resources from external sources. It has to be carefully watched that dependence of this resources is gradually declining to ensure self sustainability of the kiosks managed by the beneficiary communities.

The essence of the above suggestion is the involvement of the community in managing the ICT infrastructure that is going to bring in multifaceted benefits to them, and, in the process, to make them aware of the problem of cost-revenue balance, i.e., the problem of sustainability of the Telekiosks and the solution of the same.

4

MCTs in Honduras

Whither the Advantage of High Literacy

Background

The MCT project started in 1999, and covers five locations, namely, Valle de Angeles, Santa Lucia, Las Trojas, Montana Grande and Tegucigalpa including rural, semi-rural and urban areas. The villages selected for the study range from small hamlets of 150 people in the rural area to 4,000 people in the semi rural area.

Partnership

The MCT project is a joint effort, with the leadership of the ITU, where the communities along with national and international organizations are all active partners. The rural communities, local business persons, Rotary Club and the country's telecommunication company are the main partners.

Basic Infrastructure

The concept is built around a semi-rural MCT connected to the country's main network, and clusters of smaller rural MCTs connected to the semi-rural one by means of wireless technologies – the Spread Spectrum and Packet Radio. The MCT is the basic infrastructure for end user programmes of e-health, e-education, e-commerce, e-governance and, in general, for e-services.

New technologies such as Spread Spectrum, using non regulated frequency segments like the ones used for solutions for Office's LANs, complemented with appropriate antennas and amplifiers to cover the required distances have been used for the project. In this solution, the services convergence issue has been taken into consideration; and telephone service, by means of voice over IP (VoIP) and data flows through the same infrastructure, has been introduced. In locations like Montana Grande, the equipment is powered by solar energy. The basic infrastructure of a semi-rural MCT is as follows:

- A telecommunication link from a main MCT to the country's main network;
- 10 PCs configured as a LAN;
- Network for e-mail and web server;
- Server for rural Internet Service Provider;
- CD server for electronic library service;
- National and international telephone service;
- Facsimile, photocopy machine and PC services;
- An energy backup with up to 6 hours of autonomy.

The MCTs in rural areas have the following infrastructure:

- A telecommunication link to a main MCT using wireless technologies;
- Up to 4 PCs;
- Conventional or solar energy operation;
- Small network server with SMTP service;
- Beeper server for rural paging;
- Printer and facsimile;
- National and international telephone service by means of VoIP technologies; and
- Television set and VHS equipment.

Services

The concept of the MCT goes beyond the connectivity. The MCT is built around the concept of a "Service Mall" where the user finds, in one place, not only telecommunication, but also a set of basic public services, like, facsimile, national and international telephone service, electronic mail, web browsing, photocopy service, document printing, secretarial services, postal services, tourist information, radio communications to nearby communities, rural Internet service provision, technical expertise and training, among other services. A local web site with the main information about the area is developed in which the newcomers begin to learn the use of the Internet and its applications.

Human Resources Development and Gender Issues

The MCT project has initiated the programme of training the local people for the use of Internet and its applications such as e-mail. An e-mail address is issued free of charge to all the people of the town. Remittances by villagers settled outside the country are one of the main sources of income of the country. Therefore, the communication by e-mail, , has become one of the most popular modes. The training courses for rural women have made a difference in the acceptance of MCT at a family level.

Technology

The applications of non-traditional technologies for rural telecommunications have been tested and applied successfully. The convergence of services, incorporating data and VoIP in the same telecommunication channels, has proven to be very economical. At this very moment, the same Wireless Local Area Network technology with appropriate antennae and amplifiers is working in several remote locations; and some of them are powered by solar energy.

In the process of searching for economic solutions, a packet radio link was established to link one of the rural MCT. The narrow-band packet radio link was proven to be very versatile for text-oriented e-mail, but slow for graphic applications. The same equipment is used for the paging system.

The MCT of Montana Grande is powered by solar energy, which provides power to the telecommunication equipment, like, four PC LAN, a television and VHS equipment. Solar energy provides light for the school for the e-education programme run at night.

Sustainability

At present the pilot project is self-sustainable, and is expanding. The respective local communities operate the rural MCTs. 30% of the income from telephone calls and other PC-related services goes to the community and 70% goes to the telecommunication company. The semi-rural MCTs are, at present, operated by the government. Involvement of NGOs and community organizations for efficient management of MCTs is being given serious consideration.

Table 4.1: Cost revenue balance of the MCTs (in US$)

MCT location		2000	2001	2002	2003	2004	2005
Valle de Angeles	Revenue	10,000	16,150	15,500	14,390	14,200	13,490
	Cost	10,432	10,960	10,590	10,000	10,250	10,345
Santa Lucia	Revenue	9,650	14,870	13,150	12,430	13,100	12,330
	Cost	10,130	10,200	10,140	10,110	10,350	10,100
Las Trojas	Revenue	NA	NA	NA	650	720	930
	Cost	NA	NA	NA	473	484	493
Montana Grande	Revenue	NA	NA	NA	740	785	870
	Cost	NA	NA	NA	468	479	458

All the four MCTs in Honduras show a positive revenue balance, and this was achieved quite quickly, either in the very first year (as in the cases of Las Trojas and Montana Grande) or in the second year (Valle de Angeles and Santa Lucia). However, the important point is the social return from the project. A quick positive balance may also be accompanied with minimum social return in situations when the targeted population rarely uses the facilities.

New Applications

After the establishment of the first MCT, the project is attracting new partners with proposals for new applications. The agricultural sector and UN FAO have proposed extension of their coverage to the rural population by using the MCT infrastructure. A pilot project to incorporate the postal service using the MCT infrastructure is being explored.

The MCTs were studied to understand their functioning and also to get feedback on users and non-users of the MCT services. A description of MCTs and profiles of some of the villages and villagers they serve is privided in the following section.

MCTs Studied

The MCTs studied are located at Valle de Angeles, Santa Lucia, Las Trojas and Montaña Grande. The MCT Projects in Valle de Angeles and Santa Lucia were started in 1999 and were opened to the public in July 2000. Projects in Las Trojas and Montana Grande started in 2002 and opened to the public in 2003.

Activities under the project

MCTs in Valle de Angeles and in Santa Lucia were established with the objective of providing telephone, e-mail,

Internet access, computer facilities and services, and also to provide e-business services to the local handicraft producers. One of the objectives was to introduce the younger generation of the villages to e-mail and e-library services. A special effort was made to provide training in e-services (through seminars and classes) to the people of different social and economic backgrounds (such as, teachers, housewives, students, businessmen, government officers and religious masters).

The MCTs are located at the sites provided by the village. The buildings have been renovated with the help of the Rotary Club and the organization of Amateur Radio Operators. The site has earmarked areas for users, as well as for operational and administrative purposes. The telephone company occupies part of the administrative area and in return provide connectivity.

The MCT at Valle de Angeles is equipped with ten PCs (available for the users) and the medium size network, local area network (LAN), printer, CD service, color printer, one PC for administrative purposes and one PC for technical administration. The LAN is connected by an asynchronous modem with a 128 kbps with the national telecommunication network. The main server of LAN is also equipped with 8-telephone line interface, which, in turn, provides Internet dial-up service to thirty users. This facility provides a significant part of the income to MCT.

The concept of electronic library (e-library) was introduced through the installation of a CD server, which was able to handle up to 10 CDs at a time. Most popular programmes are the national and world geography, national and world history, mathematics, basic anatomy, etc. The MCT is equipped with a 3.5 kWatts UPS with 6 hours autonomy. It also has two telephone booths and a facsimile machine.

The MCT at Santa Lucia is equipped with six PCs configured in a LAN equipped with a local server printer, colour printer, one PC for administrative purposes and one PC for technical administration. The LAN server also is equipped with four modems, which can be accessed by 20 dial-up users of the town. The MCT is also equipped with a 3.5 kW UPS with 6 hours autonomy.

In Santa Lucia MCT, the ITU initiated the use of radio communication systems using "packet radio" technology, which allows access to the remote users by radio means. Packet radio is a technology, which allows a good bandwidth for Internet access. Together with the amateur radio community the MCT operates a Bulletin Board Server (BBS), which has more than 50 users and international link through Internet.

Las Trojas is a rather small hamlet consisting of not more than 260 inhabitants and engaged entirely in agriculture. Las Trojas is an important centre of flower and vegetable trade. The MCT introduced telephone services for the first time in the history of the hamlet. Compared to other MCT areas literacy is rather low in this area. Therefore, Internet services, were aimed mainly to the young educated people.

The MCT of Las Trojas was launched with the National Telecommunication Company, HONDUTEL, the Science and Technology Commission, COHCIT; and the World Bank.

As per the ITU suggestion, the management of MCT is being transferred to the Parents Association of the hamlet. This is an attempt to achieve sustainability. HONDUTEL, the service provider, is adjusting its tariffs in order to foster the increase of telephone service and to look for the economic viability of the service in poor rural areas. The people of Las Trojas provided the site for the operation of the MCT services. The site has been renovated with the ITU initiative together with HONDUTEL.

The equipment installed, besides the telecommunication equipment, consist of four PCs, a laser printer and a UPS. The World Bank provided the equipment and the furniture for the MCT.

ITU has initiated the use of new technologies in Las Trojas. The telecommunication link with the capital city is based on the application of WiFi technology integrating voice and data in the same channel. A few problems, regarding the use of two bands to reach the busy 2.4 GHz in the city, have been overcome by arranging repeater from the MCT to a nearby repeater on the 2.4 GHz band and from the repeater to the city on the 5.2 GHz band.

The MCT provides telephone services for national and international calls, Internet services and the use of PCs for different applications.

Montaña Grande is a small hamlet of not more than 300 inhabitants of farmers, who supply vegetables to the capital city. The MCT introduced telephone for the first time in this area. The social and economic profile is similar to that of Las Trojas, and the same national and international agencies were involved in conceptualization, management and funding of the project.

On the basis of the suggestion of HONDUTEL, the management of MCT is being transferred to the MCT Management Board of the hamlet. The MCT was installed originally in the premises of the local school, but is being shifted to a new location built by the community. The equipment installed, besides the telecommunication equipment, consist of four portable PCs, a laser jet printer and a power station operated by solar energy. The World Bank provided this equipment and furniture for the MCT.

Like in Las Trojas, connectivity has been provided by a packet radio link on the VHF band and to provide radio voice communication with MCT of Santa Lucia. The link was operable, but too slow for the users. The radio link was used for emergency situations since it has no connectivity to the national telephone network. After a trial period of six months, the packet radio link was substituted by a WiFi link.

The MCT provides telephone services for national and international calls, Internet services and the use of PCs for different applications.

Resource Mobilization

All the MCTs have been created with the partnership among multiple agencies of international, national and local levels. Following are the agencies involved under different capacities in different MCTs.

(i) ITU had provided the equipments required for all the four MCTs.

(ii) The respective townships have provided space for the projects. In the case of Montana Grande, Ministry of Public Education provided the space.

(iii) Communication services were provided by HONDUTEL.

(iv) Remodelling of MCT site was done by Rotary Club for Valle de Angeles and Santa Lucia. In the case of Las Trojas it was done by the local community, HONDUTEL and ITU.

(v) At Valle de Angeles e-library was provided by UNESCO.

(vi) In Santa Lucia, packet radio was provided by the amateur radio community.

(vii) At Las Trojas and Montana Grande, PC LAN and furniture were provided by the World Bank. The

World Bank also provided solar energy equipment for Montana Grand.

(viii) The MCTs at Las Trojas and Montana Grande needed training of the staff, which was provided by HONDUTEL.

National Level Committee for the MCT Project

The MCT projects are administered and operated by the state-owned telecommunication company HONDUTEL with the technical cooperation of ITU.

Project team

The team is composed as follows:

(a) ITU: Technical expert, administrative adviser and administrative work; and

(b) HONDUTEL: Three operational staff and one security officer.

In case of the MCT at Las Trojas and Montaña Grande respective communities provided three persons for routine activities.

Team at the project sites

In the case of Valle de Angeles and Santa Lucia two personnel are appointed for administrative functions as well as to work as the system operators. They cover two shifts from 8:00 am to 8:00 pm and provide assistance towards national and international phone calls, Internet access and teach courses related to the MCT services.

For Las Trojas and Montaña Grande, there is only one person who works both as administrator and operator. The working hours are from 9:00 am to 5:00 pm. The person provides assistance for national and international phone calls and also for Internet access.

Problems faced

There is a strong feeling that at the present level of cost-revenue structure of the MCT at Valle de Angeles and Santa Lucia, the project would function more efficiently if managed by a civil body represented by an NGO. For the MCT at Las Trojas, ITU is proposing a transfer of the administration and operation to the Parents Association of the hamlet. In the case of the MCT at Montaña Grande, the Project team is proposing a transfer of the administration and operation to the MCT Management Board of the hamlet.

Technology status and type of connectivity in the MCT and in the region around

The MCTs are located in small villages where there is no Internet service provider other than the government-operated company. The initial bandwidth assigned to the MCT was small (32 kbs) and after the users complain about the speed, it was later increased to 128 kbs.

Profile of the Villages under MCT Services

The following 11 villages (as shown in Table 4.2) around the locations of 4 MCT project were studied.

Table 4.2: Villages studied

MCT at		Villages surveyed
Valle de Angeles	:	Cerro Grande, Las Cañadas, La Cimbra, El Sunteco, and Valle de Angeles
Santa Lucia	:	Santa Lucia, Zarabanda, El Chimbo
Las Trojas	:	Las Trojas and Los Planes
Montaña Grande	:	Montaña Grande

Table 4.3 presents brief profiles of the villages.

Table 4.3: Profile of the villages

Name of village	Distance from MCT (km)	No. of household	Total population	Literacy (%)	General economic condition
Valle de Angeles	0	1,202	5,766	87	Poor
Cerro Grande	3	352	1,698	77.6	Average
Las Cañadas	5	347	1,713	85.1	Poor
La Cimbra	4	118	498	84.3	Poor
El Sunteco	3.3	130	790	84.2	Average
Santa Lucia	0	1,457	6,692	87.1	Prosperous
Zarabanda	4	194	980	84.6	Average
El Chimbo	5	475	2120	87.5	Average
Las Trojas	0	40	257	69	Poor
Los Planes	2	52	290	67	Poor
Montana Grande	0	46	275	68	Poor

Except Santa Lucia all other villages are economically backward. It is to be noted that observation on general economic condition of the village is relative with respect to the economic conditions of the villages around, or general economic condition of the country. So observation 'prosperous' only means that it is a shade better than other villages. Another important point to be noted is the high literacy rate even in the poor villages. The average family size is around five. Therefore, an overall observation is that the villages studied in Honduras are economically backward, but have significantly high literacy, and unlike many poor countries of Asia and Africa the size of the families are small.

Table 4.4 and 4.5 provide the comparative rural and remoteness of the villages in terms of the economic activities and facilities available in the villages.

Table 4.4: Economic condition of the villages – comparative ruralness

Name of s villages	Sectoral contribution (%) Agr	Minerals	H'hold industry	SME	Other	Rank
Valle de Angeles	45	0	5	10	40	1
Cerro Grande	63	1	1	0	35	3
Las Cañadas	76	12	0	0	11	8
La Cimbra	70	0	0	0	30	6
El Sunteco	68	0	5	0	27	4
Santa Lucia	49	5	0	0	46	2
Zarabanda	69	1	0	0	30	5
El Chimbo	73	2	0	0	25	7
Las Trojas	83	0	0	0	17	9
Los Planes	90	0	0	0	10	11
Montana Grande	88	0	0	0	12	10

The column 'Other' in Table 4.4 means villagers who have migrated out for varieties of jobs. 'Ruralness' is defined by the dependence on agriculture and lack of manufacturing activities in the village. If we compare Table 4.3 with Table 4.4, we can see that relative prosperity of Santa Lucia is actually because of its large percentage of population who work as migrant workers in other countries. In the absence of any significant non-agricultural economic activities within the village, migration is the second most important source of income.

Remoteness of the villages has been assessed by the location of the villages from the facilities like market, hospital, educational institute and post office. Villages have been ranked separately for all these facilities and an overall rank value is arrived at by the sum of individual rankings. Among the four MCT centres Las Trojas rank 8 out of all 11 villages. Montaña Grande and Las Trojas are fully dependent on agriculture and general economic condition is poor, even though Montaña Grande is the least remote among all 11 villages. Other two centres, namely Ville de Angeles and Santa Lucia have highest percentage of migrant workers.

Table 4.5: Economic condition of the villages – comparative remoteness

Name of village	Nearest facilities (distance in km)									
	Market	Rank	Hospital	Rank	Education Centre	Rank	Post office	Rank	Total rank value	Overall rank
Valle de Angeles	5	6	1.2	1	22	6	0.5	1	14	3
Cerro Grande	3.5	3	5	5	25	7	3.5	2	17	4
LasCañadas	5.5	8	7	7	28	9	5.5	7	31	11
La Cimbra	4.5	5	6.2	6	30	10	4.5	5	26	9
El Sunteco	3.8	4	4.9	4	26	8	3.8	3	19	6
Santa Lucia	0.3	1	7	7	14.1	4	0.5	1	13	2
Zarabanda	4.5	5	4	3	18	5	4.5	5	18	5
ElChimbo	5.2	7	9	8	9	1	5.4	6	22	7
Las Trojas	11.4	9	12	9	11.7	2	4	4	24	8
LosPlanes	12.5	10	13	10	12.5	3	4	4	27	10
Montana Grande	0.5	2	2.5	2	22	6	0.5	1	11	1

Table 4.6 shows the infrastructural facilities available in the villages under study.

Table 4.6: Infrastructure facility in the villages

Name of village	Road network	Main modes of transport	Electri-fication	Availability of electricity	Total weight	Rank
Valle de Angeles	Very good	Public/own	Full	Regular	9	1
Cerro Grande	Very good	Public/own	Full	Uncertain	8	2
LasCañadas	Very good	Public/own	Partial	Uncertain	7	3
La Cimbra	Bad	Public/own	Partial	Rare	4	4
El Sunteco	Very good	Public/own	Full	Regular	9	1
Santa Lucia	Very good	Public/own	Full	Uncertain	8	2
Zarabanda	Good	Public/own	Partial	Regular	7	3
El Chimbo	Very good	Public/own	Partial	Regular	8	2
Las Trojas	Very good	Public/own	Partial	Uncertain	8	2
Los Planes	Very good	Public/own	Partial	Uncertain	8	2
Montana Grande	Good	Public/own	Full	Regular	8	2

Four infrastructural facilities have been considered. These are: condition of road network, main modes of transport, electrification and availability of electricity. The general condition has been assessed on three-point scale; 1 for the best and 3 for the worst. Villages, more or less, share similar status on infrastructure facilities. The village La Cimbra is the poorest in terms of these facilities.

The ICT use patterns in the villages are presented in Table 4.7.

Telephone, fax, Internet and postal services are the main ICT services taken into account. Again three-point scale has been used to assess the use pattern in the villages studied. Villages were ranked according to their relative ICT use pattern. It is to be noted that the most prosperous village Santa Lucia is not the best user of ICT: it ranks third. Again El Sunteco, which ranks first in ICT use pattern, is just average in general economic condition and sixth in terms of remoteness.

Table 4.7: ICT use pattern in Villages

Name of village	Postal service	Telephone	Telefax	Internet	Total	Rank value
Valle de Angeles	Rare	Main	Main	Main	10	2
Cerro Grande	Rare	Main	Main	Main	10	2
LasCañadas	Rare	Main	Main	Main	10	2
La Cimbra	Rare	Main	Occasional	Rare	7	5
El Sunteco	Occasional	Main	Main	Main	11	1
Santa Lucia	Rare	Main	Occasional	Main	9	3
Zarabanda	Occasional	Main	Occasional	Main	10	2
El Chimbo	Occasional	Rare	Occasional	Rare	6	6
Las Trojas	Rare	Main	Rare	Main	8	4
Los Planes	Rare	Main	Rare	Main	8	4
Montana Grande	Rare	Main	Rare	Main	8	4

These are some of the observations that prompted us to try rank correlations among certain critical variables that influence the use of ICT (Table 4.8).

Notwithstanding the limitations of the exercise (small number of observations and qualitative ranking), Table 4.7 does give results that match an intuitive understanding. Literacy being more or less uniform among the villages, it was not expected to show any significant correlation with the ICT use pattern. There is also not enough variation in general economic conditions of the villages. The best coefficient is given by 'ruralness' – the extent of dependence on agriculture. Since higher the ruralness, higher is the rank value (i.e., lower is the rank), a positive rank correlation coefficient means less the ruralness (or less dependent on agriculture) better is the ICT use pattern. Access to infrastructure facilities, like having electricity is again an important determinant of the ICT use pattern. In the above exercise, this turned out to be the second most important factor governing the ICT use pattern.

Table 4.8: Rank correlations between ICT use pattern and selected socio-economic parameters

Name of villages	Access to MCT	Literacy	General economic condition	Ruralness	Remoteness	Access to facilities	Use of ICT
Valle de Angeles	1	1	3	1	3	1	2
Cerro Grande	2	3	2	3	4	2	2
LasCañadas	4	1	3	8	11	3	2
La Cimbra	3	1	3	6	9	4	5
El Sunteco	3	1	2	4	6	1	1
Santa Lucia	1	1	1	2	2	2	3
Zarabanda	3	1	2	5	5	3	2
El Chimbo	4	1	2	7	7	2	6
Las Trojas	1	3	3	9	8	2	4
Los Planes	2	3	3	11	10	2	4
Montaña Grande	1	3	3	10	1	2	4
Correlation coefficient	0.08	0.16	0.20	0.51	0.22	0.34	1

Profile of the Users and Non-users of MCT Services

The broad observations from the survey are presented in the following tables. Village-wise total number of households surveyed are given in Table 4.9.

Table 4.9: Number of household surveyed in the villages around the MCTs

Name of villages	User	Non-user
Valle de Angeles	50	50
Cerro Grande	50	50
Las Cañadas	50	50
La Cimbra	20	20
El Sunteco	20	20
Santa Lucia	50	50
Zarabanda	10	20
El Chimbo	50	50
Las Trojas	20	20
Los Planes	20	20
Montana Grande	20	20

Table 4.10 presents the sources of livelihood of the users and non-users of MCT services.

In predominantly rural areas both users and non-users have to be mainly from the farming community. That is the case in the village Los Planes. Also, most of the villages being economically dependent on agriculture, both categories are likely to be from the farming group. There is no definite pattern observable regarding occupation of the users and non-users. As we shall see later, literacy being very high in the villages, the most important barrier to access, which ICT has to overcome, is the overall economic condition of the villages and price of ICT access that determine the extent of use across the occupational groups.

Considering that age group 15–40 is most potential ICT use age group, Table 4.11 presents number of family members in this age group for the families surveyed by the study.

Table 4.10: Livelihood of the users and non-users

Name of villages	Type of family	Main source of earning			Rank	
		Farming	Business	Service	Rural	Remote
Valle de Angeles	User	12	28	10		3
	Non-user	37	8	5		
Cerro Grande	User	25	18	7	3	4
	Non-user	39	9	2		
Las Cañadas	User	15	22	13	8	11
	Non-user	39	9	2		
La Cimbra	User	15	2	3	6	9
	Non-user	18	x	2		
El Sunteco	User	12	4	4	4	6
	Non-user	18	1	1		
Santa Lucia	User	23	19	8	2	2
	Non-user	38	7	5		
Zarabanda	User	4	3	3	5	5
	Non-user	20	0	0		
El Chimbo	User	28	14	8	7	7
	Non-user	37	6	7		
Las Trojas	User	15	5	0	9	8
	Non-user	20	0	0		
Los Planes	User	20	0	0	11	10
	Non-user	20	0	0		
Montana Grande	User	14	4	2	10	1
	Non-user	20	0	0		

We have taken 15 to 40 years as the most ICT friendly age group. An expectation has been that, given the high literacy rate, number of family members in this age group will be a distinctive factor between users and non-users. The expectation does not get much support from the data. The major reason could be the poor economic condition of the villages that makes relative cost of access to ICT very high.

Table 4.12 presents data on the number of school going children in both ICT service user and non-user categories of families.

Table 4.11: Number of family members in the ICT friendly age group

Name of villages	Type of family	Number of family members in the ICT friendly age group				
		Two	Three	Four	Five	Six and more
Valle de Angeles	User	26	15	2	2	0
	Non-user	32	4	0	4	2
Cerro Grande	User	22	7	6	0	0
	Non-user	25	13	3	2	1
Las Cañadas	User	19	14	5	2	0
	Non-user	25	13	3	2	1
La Cimbra	User	9	4	0	0	0
	Non-user	13	3	2	0	0
El Sunteco	User	8	3	2	0	0
	Non-user	6	4	3	0	0
Santa Lucia	User	25	16	0	1	1
	Non-user	26	5	4	0	0
Zarabanda	User	9	3	3	0	0
	Non-user	5	6	4	0	0
El Chimbo	User	22	10	1	0	0
	Non-user	20	11	4	0	0
Las Trojas	User	3	5	4	0	0
	Non-user	3	5	5	0	0
Los Planes	User	7	3	2	1	0
	Non-user	9	3	3	1	0
Montana Grande	User	7	3	0	0	0
	Non-user	10	3	1	0	0

In this case also expectation on distinction between user and non-user families by the number of school going children did not get much support from the data.

Table 4.13 gives information on number of children going for higher education in the surveyed families.

The first three cases in Table 4.13 support the view that irrespective of rural and remoteness, families having children going for higher education is more ICT friendly. However, the observation becomes less supportive in the

Table 4.12: Number of families having school going children

Name of villages	Type of family	Number of school going children in surveyed families			
		Two	Three	Four	Five
Valle de Angeles	User	16	16	7	0
	Non-user	23	9	6	2
Cerro Grande	User	16	10	5	1
	Non-user	16	7	6	1
Las Cañadas	User	31	17	9	1
	Non-user	16	7	6	1
La Cimbra	User	13	2	0	0
	Non-user	10	2	1	0
El Sunteco	User	10	2	0	0
	Non-user	7	3	0	0
Santa Lucia	User	13	8	9	5
	Non-user	17	10	6	5
Zarabanda	User	8	6	0	0
	Non-user	8	2	1	0
El Chimbo	User	14	12	6	2
	Non-user	10	7	1	0
Las Trojas	User	7	5	0	0
	Non-user	7	7	0	0
Los Planes	User	9	6	0	0
	Non-user	5	4	0	0
Montana Grande	User	6	4	1	0
	Non-user	6	3	1	0

case of Santa Lucia which is comparatively less rural and remote but shows higher number of families having children in higher education as non-user. The distinction is much less pronounced in other cases.

The number of earning members in the surveyed families is shown in Table 4.14.

The number of earning members in the cases of these villages should not be seen as an indicator of their relative economic well-being. In fact, given the poor economic

Table 4.13: Number of families having children going for higher education

Villages	Type of family	Number of children in higher education			Total no. of family	Rank	
		One	Two	Three		Rural	Remote
Valle de Angeles	User	28	5	0	33	1	3
	Non-user	13	5	0	18		
Cerro Grande	User	12	5	0	17	3	4
	Non-user	7	6	0	13		
Las Cañadas	User	18	9	4	31	8	11
	Non-user	7	6	0	13		
La Cimbra	User	4	2	0	6	6	9
	Non-user	3	1	0	4		
El Sunteco	User	7	2	0	9	4	6
	Non-user	3	2	0	5		
Santa Lucia	User	9	8	0	17	2	2
	Non-user	15	10	0	25		
Zarabanda	User	8	1	0	9	5	5
	Non-user	4	1	0	5		
El Chimbo	User	10	4	1	15	7	7
	Non-user	7	4	1	12		
Las Trojas	User	5	1	0	6	9	8
	Non-user	4	1	0	5		
Los Planes	User	2	0	0	2	11	1C
	Non-user	4	0	0	4		
Montana Grande	User	4	1	0	5	10	1
	Non-user	5	1	0	6		

Table 4.14: Number of earning members

Name of villages	Type of families	One	Two	Three	Four	Avg.	Rank	
							Rural	Remote
Valle de Angeles	User	25	14	7	2	1.3	1	3
	Non-user	14	21	3	0	1.7		
Cerro Grande	User	27	19	0	0	2	3	4
	Non-user	17	19	4	1	1.7		
Las Cañadas	User	34	14	1	1	1.4	8	11
	Non-user	17	19	4	1	1.7		
La Cimbra	User	18	2	0	0	1.1	6	9
	Non-user	16	3	1	0	1.3		
El Sunteco	User	12	8	0	0	1.4	4	6
	Non-user	16	4	0	0	1.2		
Santa Lucia	User	21	14	10	3	2.0	2	2
	Non-user	10	33	0	3	2.0		
Zarabanda	User	13	7	0	0	1.4	5	5
	Non-user	17	3	0	0	1.2		
El Chimbo	User	31	16	0	0	1.4	7	7
	Non-user	40	9	0	0	1.2		
Las Trojas	User	15	5	0	0	1.3	9	8
	Non-user	19	1	0	0	1.0		
Los Planes	User	15	2	0	0	1.1	11	10
	Non-user	18	2	0	0	1.1		
Montana Grande	User	15	5	0	0	1.5	10	1
	Non-user	16	4	0	0	1.2		

condition of these villages, the same could be the reflection of the fact that more hands are needed to earn subsistence for a family. The average number of earning member per family of users and non-users of MCTs has been correlated with the ranking of ruralness and remoteness. For correlation between more dependence on agriculture (rural) and average number of earning members are –0.51 for users and –0.68 for non-users. When related to remoteness the figures are –0.61 and –0.34 for users and non-users, respectively. The coefficients can be interpreted as follows: the more rural the villages, less are the earning members per family. But this is much more pronounced in case of non-user families when compared to the user families. On the other hand, the more remote are the villages, less is the number of earning members per family. This is more pronounced in the case of user families. The relationship with remoteness is, however, not intuitively apparent. One possible reason could be the less job opportunities in the remote areas, and more people migrate in search of works, and hence they are more frequent users of the ICT facilities.

While interpreting these Tables, it is to be taken into consideration that much of the economic status of these villages depends on the remittances of the migrants from these villages. Similarly, much of the use of the MCT facilities also depends on the communication needs of the families with their members working outside. In Table 4.6 on ICT use pattern it is shown that Internet is the most popular mode of communication and ICT use. This is also indicative of the fact that the economy and society of the villages have strong dependence on remittances. High literacy rate enables villagers more frequent use of Internet.

Table 4.15 presents economic status of the families.

Table 4.15: Economic status of the families

Name of Village	Type of families	Economic status Higher income	Middle income	Lower income
Valle de Angeles	User	2	17	31
	Non-user	0	11	39
Cerro Grande	User	0	11	39
	Non-user	0	8	42
Las Cañadas	User	0	13	37
	Non-user	0	8	42
La Cimbra	User	0	1	19
	Non-user	0	0	20
El Sunteco	User	0	4	16
	Non-user	0	0	20
Santa Lucia	User	2	13	35
	Non-user	0	11	39
Zarabanda	User	0	6	14
	Non-user	0	0	20
El Chimbo	User	0	15	35
	Non-user	0	4	46
Las Trojas	User	0	0	20
	Non-user	0	0	20
Los Planes	User	0	0	20
	Non-user	0	0	20
Montana Grande	User	0	0	20
	Non-user	0	0	20

It is seen that both users and non-users are mainly from lower income group. The levels are comparative. It shows that the access is first constrained by their general level of poor economic conditions. Access is therefore more of a compulsion than exploration.

What do villagers think about the use of ICT? Responses of the villagers are presented in Table 4.16.

Table 4.16: Use of ICT: responses from users and non-users

Name of Village	Type of family	Main mode of Communi-cation	Main purpose of use of ICT	Perceived benefit	Suggestion
Valle de	User	1, 2	1, 2, 3, 4, 5	1, 2	1, 2, 3
Angeles	Non-user	1, 2	1, 2, 3, 4, 5	1, 2	1, 2, 3
Cerro Grande	User	1, 2	1, 2, 3, 4, 5	1, 2	1, 2, 3
	Non-user	1, 2	1, 2, 3, 4, 5	1, 2	1, 2, 3
Las Cañadas	User	1, 2	1, 2, 3, 4, 5	1, 2	1, 2, 3
	Non-user	1, 2	1, 2, 3, 4, 5	1, 2	1, 2, 3
La Cimbra	User	1, 2	1, 2, 3, 4, 5	1, 2	1, 2, 3
	Non-user	1, 2	1, 2, 3, 4, 5	1, 2	1, 2, 3
El Sunteco	User	1, 2	1, 2, 3, 4, 5	1, 2	1, 2, 3
	Non-user	1, 2	1, 2, 3, 4, 5	1, 2	1, 2, 3
Santa Lucia	User	1, 2	1, 2, 3, 4, 5	1, 2	1, 2, 3
	Non-user	1, 2	1, 2, 3, 4, 5	1, 2	1, 2, 3
Zarabanda	User	1, 2	1, 2, 3, 4, 5	1, 2	1, 2, 3
	Non-user	1, 2	1, 2, 3, 4, 5	1, 2	1, 2, 3
El Chimbo	User	1, 2	1, 2, 3, 4, 5	1, 2	1, 2, 3
	Non-user	1, 2	1, 2, 3, 4, 5	1, 2	1, 2, 3
Las Trojas	User	1, 2	1, 2, 3, 4, 5	1, 2	1, 2, 3
	Non-user	1, 2	1, 2, 3, 4, 5	1, 2	1, 2, 3
Los Planes	User	1, 2	1, 2, 3, 4, 5	1, 2	1, 2, 3
	Non-user	1, 2	1, 2, 3, 4, 5	1, 2	1, 2, 3
Montana	User	1, 2	1, 2, 3, 4, 5	1, 2	1, 2, 3
Grande	Non-user	1, 2	1, 2, 3, 4, 5	1, 2	1, 2, 3

Note: Entries mean that even if one respondent says that he uses ICT for business purposes, response is entered as use of ICT for the village of the respondent.

Main mode: 1. Telephone; 2. Internet; 3. Fax; 4. Postal services

Main Purpose: 1. Social interaction; 2. Study/education; 3. Business; 4. Profession; 5. Career Health/Hygiene; 6. Market; 7. Security; 8. Any other

Perceived benefit: 1. Social interaction; 2. Study/ education

Suggestion: 1. Lower the cost of accessing services; 2. Train people, and create awareness; 3. Better connectivity and speedier Internet connection.

Use of ICT is generally restricted to telephone and Internet. Although main purpose of the use of ICT includes business profession, etc., the main benefit perceived is social interaction and education. Lack of awareness and cost of accessing the ICT services are the major concerns of the villagers.

Observations

The villages around the four MCTs can be generally characterized as the ones having high literacy rate and negligible economic opportunities. These villages are mostly dependent on traditional agricultural practices. Lack of opportunities forced large section of the working population to look for job outside. While the villages remain poor, the available infrastructure facilities keep them remote. Therefore, the ICT facilities created under the MCT project, could not realize the potential of growth in individual enterprises. These four MCT cases of Honduras strongly suggest that MCT projects have to have a strong backing of the developmental programmes in the region. The high literacy rate particularly provides an opportunity to capitalize on the ICT services. The developmental programmes can create opportunities which, through the accessibility to ICT services, can create new enterprises, and windows to economic development.

When compared with Mali and Bhutan, it is to be discerned that they belong to the three different stages of the transformation process from marginal economy to the economy in the growth track, as we had discussed in the proposed theoretical contour. Timbuctu is a case that does not provide much opportunity either in agriculture or in non-agricultural economic activities, where infrastructure is quite inadequate for any modern economic and social activities, developmental programmes are skeletal, and literacy is very low. This is an appropriate case of marginal economy. As we have observed in the case of Timbuctu, the villages around the MCT need to be provided information that they would be able to use. These services have to be carefully developed after assessing the information needs of the people.

Bhutan, on the other hand, has reasonably settled agriculture, albeit, age old practices, and has a few modern enterprises based on local resources. Literacy is higher compared to that at Timbuctu. As the survey has shown, many people in the villages could actually articulate the type of information they need. Considering the difficult terrain and problem of accessibility through any regular transport system, access to ICT can bring in significant changes in the village life.

5

MCT Pilot Project in Vietnam

The Emergence of a New Model

Introduction

Multipurpose Community Telecentres (MCTs) in Vietnam are the ITU initiative to complement the Vietnamese government's programme for addressing the issues of social and economic development. Vietnam is an ideal choice for the initiatives for two reasons. First, all economic and social indicators rank Vietnam as a low-income country with a GDP of US$ 35.1 billion[1] in 2002, i.e. US$441 per capita (approximately US$2,070 at purchasing power parity[2]). Its human development index[3] rating is medium and it occupies the 109th position among 173 countries evaluated by UNDP in 2002. The country, therefore, provides the right case for the benefits of modern Information and Communication Technology (ICT) as a tool for economic and social development.

Secondly, the government of Vietnam is committed to reform the economic and social institutions for enacting a restructured dynamic modern economy. The current economic policy of Vietnam is based on the *Doi Moi*, the policy of economic liberalization adopted by the sixth Party Congress in 1986. The *Doi Moi* model envisages

1 Source: The World Development Indicators database; The World Bank, 2003.

2 Purchasing power parity (PPP) conversion effected by UNDP for 2002.

3 Composite index: life expectancy, adult literacy, enrolment ratio and GDP per capita expressed in terms of PPP.

developing the traditional planned economy into a market economy.

The investments effected and the growth achieved by the country, despite recent crises in Asia, show that this transition is a success. The target in 2005 was to double the GDP by 2010.

It is in this regard that ICT can provide critical support as formidable tools for diversification of economic activities and promotion of new entrepreneurial initiatives. On the one hand it can enhance public participation in the process of economic development and, on the other hand, it can make the government initiatives accessible to the citizens for economic and social development.

The MCT pilot project in Vietnam was taken up by ITU as part of the similar programmes in other countries within Buenos Aires Action Plan (BAAP) Programme No. 9—Integrated Rural Development.

Major Issues

There are three major issues involved in creating an ICT network, that is across the country, and accessible to citizens from all walks of life. The first major constraint is the technology and high capital cost associated with that. In the context of a low-income economy like Vietnam, this becomes a formidable bottleneck. Is there any techno-organizational model that can ease the bottleneck? Ultimately, the sustainability of the ICT network depends on the volume of information exchanged [uploaded and downloaded].

In an economy, that is still at a nascent stage of development, and where the market for information is yet to take shape, economic and social group-specific content development with a view to attracting large segments of an uninitiated population and enabling their access to information and communication services, becomes the second critical issue.

The third important issue is intrinsic to the target population. The information needs of the people dependent on traditional economic and social practices are limited to a bare minimum, and definitely will not stretch to the extent of paying money to acquire information. This is particularly true of nations where the economy is not fully monetized, as in the case of economies highly dependent on traditional agricultural practices. The creation of ICT facilities for such a set of population does not automatically lead to the use of the facility, unless it is associated with ongoing developmental initiative coupled with effective awareness-development programmes, to promote the accentuated use of information in economic and social activities.

These are some of the issues that the present evaluation report has attempted to discuss in the light of the Vietnam experience.

> **Issues for evaluation**
>
> Demand for ICT, is derived from the information intensity of the society. Information intensity, inturn, depends on the state of development of the economy. Therefore, MCT services, have to be **accessible** (in terms of technology and price configuration), and is **access worthy** (in terms of content), and has to be associated with awareness development programmes to enable **accentuated** use of information, keeping pace with social and economic changes.

Source of Information

Much of the technical information has been collected from secondary sources and supplemented with information gathered during our visits to the site and from discussions with the project authorities. However, the core information for the report is based on the information obtained from field visits and discussion with post and telecom office personnel in the four MCT areas and also with the President and other PTIT staff members associated directly with the MCT pilot project. The PTIT was also provided with a structured questionnaire for a survey among the users and non-users of the MCT facilities in all four locations.

The data, made available after the survey, were at aggregated level. We have tried to make best use of the data by supplementing them with field interviews and critical views gathered during intensive discussion with the users and project staff at both field and PTIT HQ levels.

The mission was concluded with an evaluation meeting at Hanoi, which brought together representatives of ITU, the Ministry of Posts and Telematics (MPT), Ministry of Science and Technology (MoST), Ministry of Culture and Information (MCI), Ministry of Agriculture and Rural Development (MARD), Ministry of Health (MoH), the Vietnam Posts and Telecommunications Corporations (VNPT), PTIT, the Research Institute of Posts and Telecommunications (RIPT), Dak Lak/Dak Nang Telecom, the Bac Giang and Bac Ninh P&Ts and the Krongpak Hospital. The meeting fostered enlightened discussion on the future of the project, its replicability, weaknesses and achievements. The present report has greatly benefited from this discussion and used input from various presentations made at the occasion.

Brief Description of the MCT Project in Vietnam

Much of the success of the MCT pilot project depends on its ability to continuously diversify its services to cater to the varied needs of the target group. A basic characteristic of a rural and remote economy is the lack of diversification of its economic activities. It is, therefore, expected that MCTs be initially used only for basic ICT services. In the case of

Vietnam, because of the high literacy rate among younger generation, acceptance of many information services is likely to grow very fast, not only in terms of information exchange but also for search for information. The MCTs in Vietnam will have to be highly proactive so as to retain their character as a premium ICT-based service provider. This section will briefly describe the services provided by MCTs and the organizational arrangements put in place to enable them. One important aspect of the pilot project is to monitor impact and develop suitable indicators for comparability with similar projects in other countries. This essential task for the consolidation of knowledge, pertaining to sustainability and replicability, will also be described in this section along with project implementation (including organizational arrangements and the respective responsibilities of partners).

Specific Services to be provided by MCTs in Vietnam

After a review of the socio-economic conditions and existing telecom infrastructure, four sites were selected for MCT pilot projects. Two MCTs were set up - one at the town of Krong Pak and the other at Eaphe commune in the central-Western mountainous area of the Dak Lak province. Other two were set up at Tan An and Dong Quang communes of the former Ha Bac province.

From the available project document and also from the presentations made by the project authorities in Vietnam we restate the services that have been envisaged to be provided by all the four MCTs:

- **Information services:** In addition to providing normal post and telecommunication services, MCTs were to become a hub of information on government declarations, policies, regulation, etc. They were also to provide information on health, environment, culture and tourism. For professionals, MCTs were to be equipped with information on jobs available and skill profiles of the local workers, along with training and education opportunities.

- **Business support centre:** MCTs were expected to become business support centres for professionals, SMEs and local authorities. Services that were considered essential to attract professionals and entrepreneurs were: access to modern ICT facilities (telephone, fax, e-mail, internet, printing, scanning and PC support) along with secretarial support and training on the use of ICT. Gradually, MCTs were to emerge as "Knowledge Networks" to provide information and training on improved methods of agriculture, animal husbandry, horticulture and similar activities relevant to the needs of local economic activities. They could also extend services to local businesses on management, accounting, taxation, etc. and become a virtual market place by providing market-related information and promoting the sale and purchase of local products through the use of Internet.
- **Educational services:** MCTs were to develop services for augmenting adult literacy programmes, training of teachers at different levels, professional skill development and training of farmers and health workers. It has been felt that, to extend services in this direction MCTs have to work in close collaboration with universities and other training organizations (national as well as international) for curriculum development and also for development of suitable platform and technologies for distance learning through computer networks.
- **Tele-medicine:** MCTs were envisaged to develop network connectivity with local, provincial, national and international level hospitals for making remote diagnosis and distance training of the local health

workers possible. This would also facilitate the exchange of information of various medical tests and enable access to appropriate medical advice for the people in remote and rural areas.

- **Video production and rental:** MCTs would actively encourage the production of video programmes with local content and their rental by the local population.

Impact Evaluation of MCTs

The evaluation of MCTs with regard to sustainability and replicability remained one of the central issues. It has been envisaged that through the pilot project some of these issues would be further enunciated. It was, therefore, expected that the four MCTs in Vietnam would help development of a model for partnership for resource mobilization and sustainability. The development of adequate content for the afore-mentioned services would require a critical assessment of the local needs and the cooperation of local populations, enterprises, local and national authorities and organizations. The MCT experience was expected to throw light on the process of involvement of different economic and social sectors, and different government and private agencies in evolving appropriate services and organizational structure for deriving benefits attuned to ensuing changes in economic and social lives of the regions.

The impact of MCTs on different user groups has to be closely monitored through a comprehensive evaluation of social, economic and cultural aspects of the region, with a view to contributing to the development of comparable evaluation methodology and indicators.

Project Implementation Team

Dr. Phung Van Van, President of PTIT, headed the implementation team of the project as National Project Coordinator. He was supported by Dr. Nguyen Minh Dan,

Director of RIPT, as infrastructure team Coordinator, and Dr. Nguyen Quy Minh Hien, Head, Department of Telecom Network, RIPT, as the team Leader.

The following four application-oriented sub-teams were constituted for overseeing the aforementioned activities:

(i) The Tele-medicine Application Team, led by Dr. Pham Hung Chung, Director of the Traditional Medicine Department, MoH;

(ii) The Culture and Education Application Team, led by Mr. Pham The Khang, Director of the Library Department, MCI, with Ma Vuong Thanh Huong, Director of the Centre for Education Information, National Institute for Education Development, Ministry of Education and Training (MET), as Assistant Team Leader.

(iii) The Small and Medium Enterprise Application Team, led by Dr. Ta Ba Hung, Director of the National Centre for Scientific and Technological Information and Documentation, MoST;

(iv) The Agriculture and Rural Development Application Team, led by Dr. Ma Chuong Tho, Deputy Director of the Department for Resettlement and Development of NEZs, MARD.

All the four MCTs were, therefore, equipped with following equipment:

- One computer system consisting of one server, one notebook, 10 PCs, 11 UPS, one CD-writer;
- One hub and network appliances;
- One 56K modem;
- One laser printer and one colour printer;
- One scanner;
- One digital camera;

- One digital video recorder;
- One digital audio recorder;
- One projector with screen;
- One photocopier;
- One 29 colour TV;
- One DVD.

The MCTs in Eaphe and Krong Pak were connected with nxISDN 2B+D connections and the ones in Bac Ninh and Bac Giang were connected with both high-speed ADSL and ISDN connections.

Implementation Trajectory of MCT Pilot Project in Vietnam

From conceptualization to actual implementation of the project involving multiple national and international agencies, it was a long winding process to arrive at a point when flow of services began. Below is a chronological outline of the work carried out to implement the four MCTs in Vietnam.

A draft project proposal was prepared by ITU and an agreement signed between the ITU and Director General of Post and Telematics (DGPT). The project document was based on a feasibility study and extensive consultations amongst various national agencies. The VNPT was given the responsibility to carry out the first phase of the project, namely setting up of two MCTs in the Dak Lak province. Four Application teams and one Infrastructure team were set up and the National Project Coordinator was appointed.

The project had a setback at this stage. There were a few transfers of staffs at different levels in the organizations that were to be directly involved in the implementation of the project. As a result, the project was delayed by almost two years. The project finally began in early 2000, following a review of the financial status and fresh implementation plan.

Buildings for MCTs were completed in Dak Lak by early 2001. Office and telecom equipment were procured. Books and other material for creation of library facilities were obtained. The next two years saw the MCTs open in Bac Ninh and Bac Giang. The MCTs in Dak Lak formally opened to the public, offering basic postal and ICT services, including Internet and a reading room. An intensive training programme in both technical and business issues of running the MCTs was organized. The MCT team also went on a study visit to Sweden for exposure to different models service provision and utilization.

All the four MCTs are currently operational and providing basic ICT services to the local populations. An ITU expert team visited three MCTs and interacted with the users and P&T officials at the project sites and at Hanoi.

Cost-revenue Balance Sheet of MCTs

At the time of the evaluation the MCTs in Vietnam had been operational roughly for two years. In a region of low level of ICT density a period of two years is too short a time for all the projected services of MCTs to mature. Popularization of MCT services is a gradual process and it depends on the shaping of the economic activities around the MCTs and requires coordination collaboration and cooperation among various local and national level stakeholders.

Another typical and well-recognized characteristic of ICT is that it involves high capital cost, and needs a large customer base for its sustainability. Prices for ICT services have to be low enough to become affordable to the rural and remote economy of resource-poor country like Vietnam. The prices can become substantially lower when the customer base is large enough. All resource-poor countries face this circularity of the problem when introducing ICT-based services. Two important policies through which this problem is addressed are: (a) subsidised services, and (b) resource mobilization to fund the subsidy.

Capital and Operational Cost of MCT

In the case of four MCTs in Vietnam, revenue earned over two years was hardly matching the cost. At the same time, there was noticeable improvement in revenue earning in the later year. This indicates a general acceptance of the MCT services and points to a possible enlargement of the customer-base in the near future.

Table 5.1 presents the cost scenario of 4 MCTs for both capital cost and operational cost. Capital cost is higher for Dak Lak and Krong Pak, as new facilities had to be built to house the MCTs.

Revenue Base of MCT

Table 5.2 shows the revenue base of the MCT services for two years of operation. It is evident from the Table 5.2 that MCTs are providing only basic ICT services. Other projected services had not by then developed enough to contribute to revenues. Fax services are not in use at all, in none of the MCTs. Since the extent of use of ICT services is directly related to the exposure of the economy to market exchanges, limited use of MCT services indicates that the economies around MCTs are not exposed enough to commercialization and the market forces. The demand for Value-added services is likely to increase when these economies become more diversified and more dependent on exports and imports. Table 5.2 also shows that the rates for basic ICT services like Mobile and Internet have substantially declined from the year 2003 to 2004, and the declines are closely associated the with rise in use of both the services in terms of hour.

Table 5.1: Cost of establishing and running MCTs at the four locations

Year	Capital cost (in mln. VND)			Operational cost (in mln. VND)			
	Equipment	Furniture	Other	Electricity	Water	Wage	Other
MCT				**Krong Pak**			
2002	426.44 + US$ 1.44	-	-	-	-	-	-
2003				7.50	0.33	17.50	2.00
2004				9.00	0.36	19.20	2.40
MCT				**Dak Lak**			
2002	426.44 + US$ 1.44	-	-	-	-	-	-
2003				4.50	0.18	9.50	1.20
2004				8.00	0.30	19.00	1.20
MCT				**Bac Giang**			
2002	461.80	9.00	5.30	-		-	-
2003	-	-	-	28.80 (includes water)	-	30.00	12.00
2004	-	-	-	28.80		30.00	12.00
MCT				**Bac Ninh**			
2002	456.00	-	-	-		-	-
2003				28.80	15.00	12.00	18.80
2004				28.80	14.00	12.00	18.80

Source: Information provided by PTIT on the basis of responses to the questionnaire

Table 5.2: Extent of use of the four MCT services at ruling rates

Year		Cost of services and extent of use				
		Land line	Mobile		Fax	Internet
			Local	National		
Rates	2003	770 /mt.	1800/mt	2700/mt	-	4500/ 1hr
(in VND)	2004	770 /mt.	850/30s.	1200/30s	-	3000/ 1hr
			Use in time units			
MCT			**Krong Pak**			
	2003	14000 mts. Land line + mobile			-	3000 hrs*
	2004	17000 mts Land line + mobile			-	3200 hrs*
MCT			**Dak Lak**			
	2003	13000 mts Land line + mobile			-	1700 hrs*
	2004	16500 mts Land line + mobile			-	3000 hrs*
MCT			**Bac Giang**			
	2003		Not available		-	5600 hrs*
	2004		Not available		-	6400 hrs*
MCT			**Bac Ninh**			
	2003		Not available		-	NA
	2004		Not available		-	NA

* Figures are close approximates.

Source: Information provided by PTIT on the basis of responses to the questionnaire

Revenue-cost Balance

Table 5.3 presents the number of users of the MCT facilities and compares the revenue earned with costs incurred. Only the Bac Ninh MCT was able to provide cost data with amortization costs, revealing a wide gap between cost and revenue. The same procedure could be used by other MCTs to estimate their respective gaps. It is also to be noted that the revenue from telephone and Internet services alone could exceed the running cost of the MCTs. Revenue-cost scenario is likely to improve, once other services become operational.

It is evident from Table 5.3 that MCTs are, presently, neither fully operational nor sustainable. However, the issue of sustainability and the associated issue of replicability, are further addressed separately.

Table 5.3: Extent of use and revenue earned from MCT services

Year	No. of users			Revenue	Running cost
	Telephone	Fax	Internet	(min VND)	(min VND)
MCT			**Krong Pak**		
2003	5250	-	235	-	
2004	6180			90.00	31.00 (without amortization)
MCT			**Dak Lak**		
2003	5120	-	175	-	
2004	5970	-	217	82.00	30.00 (without amortization)
MCT			**Bac Giang**		
2003	3500	50	2300	25.20 (Internet)	70.00 (without amortization)
2004	4100	75	2600	19.20 (Internet)	70.00 (without amortization)
MCT			**Bac Ninh**		
2003		10510		27.00	107.18 (amortization)
2004		15670		33.00	110.59 (amortization)

Source: Information provided by PTIT on the basis of responses to the questionnaire

Telecom Network Performance

Vietnam's telephone network has grown at a sustained pace in recent years, rapidly integrating the most advanced technologies.

The entire network has been digitized. Over a million new lines were installed in 2001. The overall density of the network, in 2005, stands at 18.73 lines per 100 inhabitants. 90% of the communes are connected to the national network.

Considerable efforts are being made to deploy the fixed network. Between 1991 and 1998, the fixed-line density grew thirteen-fold. In 2000–2005, Vietnam's teledensity growth rate was the highest in the world. Vietnam is better equipped than other low-income countries, which have an average overall teledensity of 3.87 fixed or mobile lines per 100 inhabitants. This performance is all the more remarkable because of the fact that Vietnam's per capita GDP in 2000 (US$ 393) was lower than the average for those same countries (US$ 432). By 2005 per capita GDP of Vietnam became US$ 650 and matched the telecom growth.

The telecom regulatory framework of Vietnam recognizes information technology as the most potential contributor to economic and social development and hence proposes the use of IT to touch every economic sector, to introduce state-of-the-art technology into the national information network and also to develop the IT industry for employment and wealth generation.

These objectives would be achieved through:

- Technically upgrading the telecommunication and Internet infrastructures for attaining regional standards in respect of coverage, quality and cost.
- Developing a seed bed of technical skills (including 50,000 technical experts with university degrees).
- Developing the software industry (with a target of US$ 500 million turnover, or 4% of the Vietnamese GDP in 2005).
- Developing the hardware industry (with a target of US$ 1 billion turnover by 2005).

Telecom Infrastructure in Vietnam

All the towns, provinces and districts of the country are equipped with digital switching systems. The switches are interconnected by microwave, optical fibre or VSAT systems. An optical fibre north-south link with a data rate of 34 Mbit/s is partially duplicated by a second link installed on the high-voltage power line connecting Hanoi to Ho Chi Minh City.

Submarine cables

There are several international submarine links, the three main ones being the following:

- TVH, connecting Thailand, Vietnam and Hong Kong;
- CSC, which will eventually connect five countries (China, Laos, Malaysia, Singapore and Thailand), in addition to Vietnam; and
- SEA-ME-WE 3, in which VNPT has invested US$ 33 million.

Satellite transmissions

Vietnam uses various foreign satellites positioned in its area. A VSAT system was installed in October 1996 by VTI and Telstra. The system uses the Asiasat-2 satellite and provides all kinds of telecommunication services, mainly for the oil and gas industries.

There are currently seven satellite-receiving earth stations, distributed as follows:

- Three in Ho Chi Minh City;
- Two in Hanoi;
- One in Danang;
- One in Song Be.

Structure of the Sector

The telecom regulatory body was restructured in 1993, creating the Department-General of Posts and Telecommunications (DGPT) under the MPT, with the VNPT as its operating arm.

As a part of the process of liberalization, DGPT has granted four more licences to new Vietnamese operators; namely, Vietel [under the supervision of the Ministry of Defence (MoD)], Saigon Postel (partially owned by VNPT), ETC (a subsidiary of Vietnam Electricity) and Vishipel (an entity controlled by the Vietnamese Navy).

Operators

The VNPT is the main Vietnamese player in the posts and telecommunication sector. It manages all networks and services and controls a number of subsidiaries providing telecommunication services, such as

- VTI for international communications;
- VTN for the domestic network;
- VDC for packet-switched data transmission and the Internet; and
- VMS and Vinaphone for GSM.

The VNPT also administers several major investment projects, including VINASAT, rural telephony, increase in the capacity of exchanges and switching centres, laying of optical fibre cables (terrestrial and maritime), strengthening of Internet services and mobile telephony.

Universal access

The rural telecommunication development programme for the provinces is a non profit initiative targeting rural areas and ethnic minorities. An extensive programme of posts and telecommunication Cultural Points was launched in 1998, with the aim to provide basic services to the commune. It is envisaged that, by 2005, all communes will be served by Cultural Points.

Fixed telephony

In 2001, Vietel was the first fixed telephony operator to use voice over IP technology, thus reducing long-distance tariffs.

The other operators, like VNPT, Saigon Postel, ETC and Vishiptel, now also have a presence in this segment, providing customers with domestic and international communication services at competitive prices.

After VNPT, Saigon Postel was the second operator authorized to build its own fixed-telephony network, covering only the metropolitan area of Ho Chi Minh City in the initial phase.

Teledensity reached a level of 19 fixed lines per 100 inhabitants in 2005, which is to say nearly twice the average for low-income countries. The annual increase in subscriptions is also substantial at 26%, which is twice the average and one of the fastest rates for this category among low income countries. In 2002, VNPT achieved a turnover of more than US$ 1.3 billion (compared with US$ 1.079 billion in 2000) and reached 5.4 million installed lines. The growth forecasts for 2005, thus, have been well exceeded.

Mobile telephony

In 2001, nearly 30% of Vietnamese subscribers had opted for mobile telephony. Mobile teledensity in 2001 was 1.54 lines per 100 inhabitants, which was once again higher than the average level of around 0.95 lines among the low income countries. The penetration rate is currently reported to be 2%. Between 1995 and 2001, the annual growth rate of mobile telephony (94%) was close to the observed average (92.3%). In 2005 number of mobile phone subscriber was 10.68 per 100 inhabitants.

The VMS and Vinaphone, both controlled by VNPT, are the two operators using the GSM standard. The VMS has been developed under the Mobifone brand, following the signature in 1995 of a cooperation contract between VNPT and the Swedish company Comvik. The contract was worth nearly US$ 130 million. Vinaphone is fully controlled by the Vietnam Telecom Services Company, an affiliate of VNPT.

Today, all of Vietnam's 61 provinces of have cellular network coverage, albeit only partial in some cases. Vietnamese users may also utilize their mobile telephones in over 30 foreign countries, thanks to agreements signed with other operators.

Vietel and ETC could negotiate technological and financial alliances with foreign operators in order to position themselves also in the mobile telephony segment.

Telecom Infrastructure in MCTs

Among the four MCTs, each one at Bac Ninh and Bac Giang have the most advanced telecommunication network. The Bac Ninh province has digital switch system to serve the whole province with the installed capacity of 100,000 lines. The optical cable system connects the whole province ensuring high quality transmission and bandwidth for national and international telecommunication services.

Both Bac Ninh and Bac Giang have high-speed internet connections through ADSL and NGN technologies. Both Krong Pak and Ea Phe, in Dak Lak province, have nxISDN 2B+D connections. The available telecom infrastructure is, therefore, adequate for the projected services of MCTs.

The technical solution and network designed for connectivity at MCTs detailed in the technical report are summarized below. They were planned to support and enable the provision of the following services:

- Telephone, fax and post services;
- Library services providing magazines, books, newspapers, CD, video and audiotapes;
- Local information and Internet access;
- Tele-education and training;
- Tele-medicine.

The hardware requirements were:

- PC, Laptop;
- Server + LAN;
- Camcorder, photocopier, digital camera, colour printer, laser printer, projector;
- Table, chair and other facilities.

The network requirements were:

- LAN: *using* equipments such as servers, PC, laptop, switch and hub to enable customer access to local information.
- Telecom connection*:* using broadband connections for video-conference, tele-education and Internet access.

Two MCTs, using nxISDN 2B+D connections at Eaphe and KrongPak, were to be set up in phase one. These MCTs were to be connected with each other and also with other relevant organizations (like university, hospital, etc.) through Ban Me Thuat exchange to make them ready to provide projected services. The network established in two MCTs in Phase one is shown in Fig. 5.1.

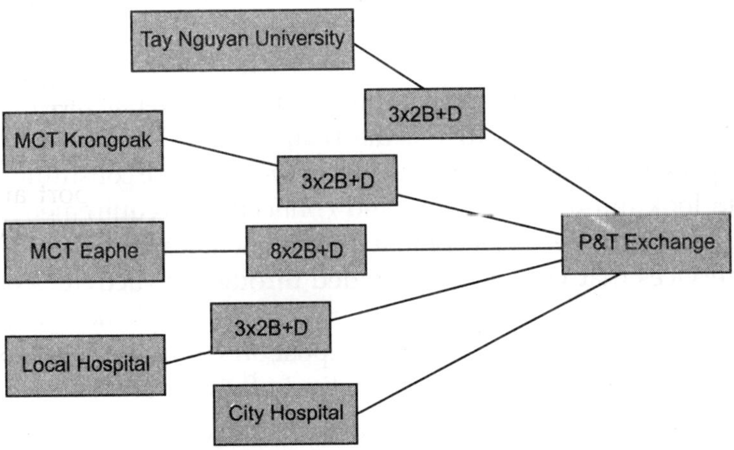

Fig. 5.1*:* Networking in phase 1
Source: Technical report presented by the PTIT technical team at the evaluation meeting (Hanoi, 19 April 2005).

The Phase two was for establishing two MCTs at Bac Giang and Bac Ninh using both ADSL and ISDN connections.The network connection was established using ADSL for Dong Quang MCT and nxISDN for Tan An MCT. The set up was, therefore, well equipped for providing technical support to the projected MCT services.

Future Telecom Infrastructure for MCTs

The expected increase in traffic as well as in demand for improved quality services will require technological and infrastructural upgrades. The PTIT has proposed to use xDSL connections for all the MCTs (one line each for Internet and conference) and to further invest on equipment such as MCU, VCS, router, server, etc. for facilitating the establishment of multi-point video-conferences between MCTs and other relevant organizations. The proposed future network solution is shown in Fig 5.2.

Effectiveness of Organization

The PTIT has been entrusted with the main responsibility for the implementation of the project. The President of PTIT was appointed National Coordinator of the project. He was to be supported by the Director of RIPT as infrastructure Team coordinator, and by the Head of the Department of Telecom Network, RIPT as the Team Leader. The VNPT set up teams for application and infrastructure were constituted to look into the hardware and connectivity requirements, and also the needs for content development for the projected services that were to be provided through the activities of MCTs. Because of the involvement of VNPT, implementation of the projects through regional post offices in the selected project sites became administratively feasible and smooth.

By 2003, both Phase one and Phase two had been completed and MCTs were fully operational, offering post office services, telephone services and Internet services.

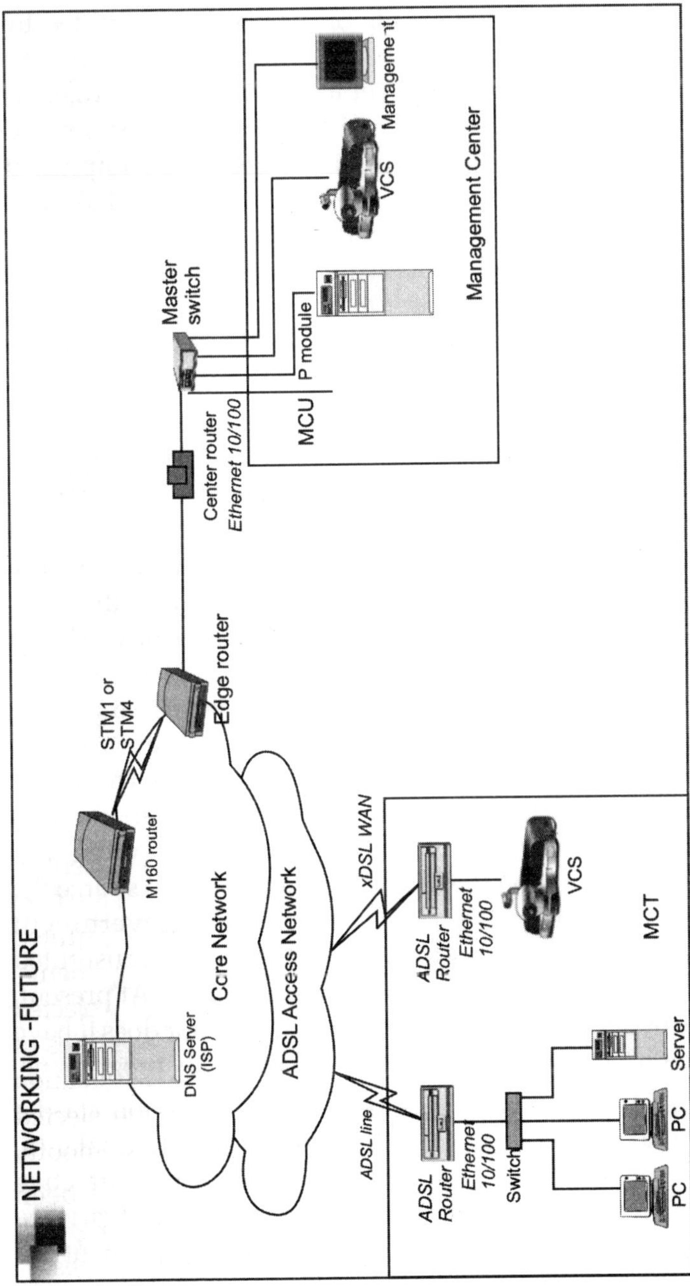

Fig. 5.2: Proposed future network
Source: Technical solution report presented by the PTIT technical team at the evaluation meeting (Hanoi, 19 April 2005)

Table 5.8 gives the details of the services provided by MCTs. Table 5.8 when compared with Table 5.2, gives the clear picture that MCTs are yet to provide all the projected and potential services. Discussion with the Directors and other staffs of the P&T offices indicated a few important areas that needed attention. Regarding services like tele-medicine, and tele-education and similar other services, they thought that various government offices whose active support was needed, could not be brought together to work in a coordinated manner. As a result, the four-application teams could not provide the expected services.

Inter-departmental coordination remains the weakest aspect of the management of MCTs in Vietnam. It appears that the application teams have to have adequate support and authority from the respective departments to plan and coordinate the programme. One way of achieving the necessary coordination is to extend and strengthen the team, drawing people from departments which have direct relevance to the 'applications' that are to be developed. Let us take the example of SME application team. Team leader is the Director of National Centre for Scientific and Technological Information and Documentation. The leader has to have, on the one hand enough organizational and financial resources to plan and design the content and connectivity, and on the other hand, authority to source the required information from the relevant government departments. Ideally, the team should have been constituted of personnel from all the relevant departments. At present, the team does not have any other members, nor does it have any defined authority to design and execute any programme.

This is one area where private participation can be gainfully used. We have seen that the cost-revenue balance, at the present stage of operation of MCTs, is not attractive enough for private enterprises. Involvement of private enterprises for content development may complement the expertise of application teams constituted of personnel from government departments. Private participation may also bring two definite benefits: (i) the capability building of local enterprises in new opportunities with high income and employment potential, and (ii) attracting investment of the private enterprise in the business of MCT through the learning experience from their involvement in the programme.

It was also suggested in the evaluation meeting in Hanoi that ITU or funding agencies should allocate separate fund for application development and technical help for designing the content and connectivity. While this suggestion appeared reasonable, the organizational arrangements for application development were needed to be revamped immediately to derive full potential of the expected benefits from MCTs. The private enterprises that are likely to partner the application development programme should be allowed and helped to enter appropriate collaboration with similar enterprises from other countries. The team should also have exposure to the similar programmes in other developing countries like India where projects like e-choupal under private initiative have shown the potential use of ICT for development of rural economy.

Another aspect that emerged time and again during several discussion at different levels is the use of 'state-of-the-art technology' in MCTs and the cost associated with it. The question is directly related to the sustainability of MCTs. General suggestion was in favour of a scaled down version of MCT and much simpler organizational structure, having scope of gradual improvement in the services as the economy and society become more tuned to gainful use of information.

Survey of Users and Non-users

A questionnaire-based survey was conducted in the villages served by four MCTs. It was conducted by the staff of PTIT.

The questionnaire had three components. The first component was to gather information mostly on the present status of the project in terms of services being provided, extent of use of the facilities by the local people, identification of the impediments in delivering the projected services, and also cost and revenue profiles. Most of this information were available from the local project authorities.

The second part of the questionnaire was for the project authorities at the national and local level to account for their assessment and experience about the outcome and management of the project, and suggestions there on for its sustainability and replicability.

The third part of the questionnaire was intended to identify and understand the factors that can discriminate between users and non-users of MCT facilities. It is to be noted here that by 'non-users' we mean non-users of MCT facilities, and not non-users of ICT. The survey was designed to examine the social and economic discriminants between users and non-users of MCT facilities.

Coverage of the Survey

Information gathered through the first two components have been used in Section 3 to substantiate an overview of the project's cost-revenue status. The findings of the third component are summarized in Table 5.4.

Table 5.4: Respondent structure of the survey

MCTs	No. of villages served	No. of villages surveyed	No. of households in the villages		No. of respondents	
			Max	Min	User	Non-user
Krong Pak	6	3	3850	217	80	80
Dak Lak	6	3	536	235	120	90
Bac Giang	13	13	270	73	25	35
Bac Ninh	5	3	-	-	40	15
Total	30	22	-	-	265	230

Comparative 'ruralness' of the villages

One of the objectives of the survey has been to develop measurable indicators for 'rural' and 'remote' areas and examine the association of use of ICT and MCT with the degree of 'ruralness' and 'remoteness'. We have used simple comparative definition of 'ruralness' in terms of four measurable factors, namely, literacy, dependence on agriculture, household industry and dependence on SMEs. Table 5.5 presents the comparative information for the villages surveyed.

It is to be noted that the figures shown in the columns grouped under "Occupation" do not add up to 100%, as they exclude segments of users engaged in professional activities such as teaching and government jobs.

Table 5.5 indicates that Bac Ninh province is comparatively more industrialized, having about 40% population dependent on agriculture and 5% on household industries. The economic scenario of the province is one of growing dependence on industries. Growing industrialization of the area is distinctively visible along the highway dotted on both sides with new industrial units. The province has highest industrial growth rate in Vietnam. Large number of small enterprises is coming up all around the province. The local authority has a programme of developing it as an industrial hub by 2015.

The Bac Giang province is also an upcoming industrial area. The province has good number of traditional handicraft units, mostly wood crafting, having international markets. Many of them have large showrooms downtown and also have marketing arrangements through their own websites.

Villages in Dak Lak, on the contrary, are almost fully dependent on agriculture with marginal presence of some household-based handicraft units. Similar is the condition of the two villages in Krogan Pak area, barring Phuoc An,

Table 5.5: Comparative ruralness of the villages studied

MCTs	Villages surveyed (Household, Population)	Literacy (%)	Occupation (% household) Agriculture	Household industry	SME	Ruralness
Krong Pak	Phuoc An* (3850, 19685)	98	60	15	23	6
	Zung B (310, 1780)	90	90	5	-	1
	Ban (217, 1294)	90	90	5	-	1
Dak Lak	Buon Phe (225, 1194)	95	90	5	3	3
	Phuoc Hoa (665, 3789)	98	80	18	-	2
	Phroc Loe (536, 2321)	90	85	10	3	4
Bac Giang**	13 Villages (Household no. Max 270 and Min 88) (Population Max 1125 and Min 330)	98	60	18	20	5
Bac Ninh***	Dong Quang	98	40	5	53	7
	Dong Ky	98	40	5	53	7
	Phu khe	97	40	5	53	7

Notes: * Sub-districts have better facilities and more non-agricultural activities than other villages.

** Upcoming industrial district with good numbers of small hamlets, most of which have small and tiny industrial units.

*** Growing industrial district.

which is actually a sub-district and has substantial number of small enterprises and traditional household industries.

If we define ruralness of an economy in terms of its relative dependence on traditional agriculture, we can rank the aforesaid villages as shown in the last column of Table 5.5.

This classification is quite loose and is applicable when dealing with small number of cases. The thumb-rule applied was to establish the first cut-off point as dependence on traditional agriculture, followed by dependence on household industries, followed by dependence on SMEs, etc. The problems encountered in ranking three Dak Lak villages was resolved by giving higher weight to the number of SMEs over the number of traditional household industries. Hence, in spite of showing a higher dependence on agriculture (90%) than Phuoc Hoa (80%), Buon Phe is considered more industrialized by virtue of its 3% dependence rate on SMEs, as opposed to non-significant figures for Phuoc Hoa. Finally, it may be noted that literacy rates were not considered in this exercise, as the rates in all villages surveyed are more or less the same.

In brief the villages were ranked separately for all the three factors, and then three ranks were added up for each village to arrive at the total rank value. All factors were given equal weightage. Final ranking, as shown in Table 5.5, was arrived at by comparing total rank values for all villages.

The basic distinction among the provinces is the presence of increasing number of SMEs. It is a rise in the large number of small enterprises which is the hallmark of the economic transformation of these provinces. Rise in the individual enterprises has been argued as one of the important dimension of change which the use of information brings in. Access to information, in the presence of high rate of literacy, has enabled the people to create their own individual enterprises. This is what has contributed to the transformation process of the economies of these provinces.

Comparative Remoteness of the Villages

Remoteness has been similarly defined in relation to (a) distance from the nearest town, and (b) availability of infrastructure facilities. Table 5.6 shows the distances of various civic facilities from the villages, including data on markets, hospitals, higher education centres and post offices.

The villages have been ranked under each category according to their distances . Rank values under each of these categories have been added up to obtain the overall rank value and the final rank value. All facilities have been given equal weightage.

Comparative Usability of Facilities

The same procedure has been used for Table 5.7, which compares different civic facilities in terms of usability. The villages were ranked separately on all factors (all of which have the same weightage), and then the values were added up to obtain the total ranked value and a final ranking, (in the last column of Table 5.7). The villages are ranked in terms of rural and remoteness as given in Tables 5.5–5.7. However, these figures do not explain the ICT use patterns of the villagers. Table 5.8 displays the data obtained with regard to the extent and type of ICT services used by the targeted villagers.

ICT Services Used by Villagers

Table 5.8 has been prepared from the responses of the villagers in terms of 'mainly', 'occasionally', and 'rarely' for the use of services such as postal, telephone, fax, Internet, and mobile. Like preceding tables, we have given same weightage for all the services. This means that no distinction

Table 5.6: Comparative remoteness of the villages

Villages surveyed (Household, Population)	Distance of various facilities (km) MCT	Market	Hospital (Rank)	Higher edn. (Rank)	Post office Centre (Rank)	Overall rank (Rank)	Final rank
Phuoc An (3850, 19685)	0.5 (1)	0.2 (1)	0.5 (1)	33 (4)	0.3 (1)	8	1
Zung B (310, 1780)	2.5 (5)	1.0 (3)	0.5 (1)	40 (5)	0.3 (1)	15	6
Ban (217, 1294)	2.1 (4)	3.0 (5)	2.5 (4)	31 (3)	1 (3)	19	7
Buon Phe (225, 1194)	0.5 (1)	0.5 (2)	0.5 (1)	41 (6)	0.5 (2)	12	4
Phuoc Hoa (665, 3789)	2.0 (3)	1.0 (3)	1.5 (3)	43 (7)	1.5 (4)	20	8
Phroc Loe (536, 2321)	0.5 (1)	0.5 (2)	1.5 (3)	40 (5)	0.5 (2)	13	5
13 Villagesof Bac Giang	Av g 1.5 (2)	0.2–1.0 (3)	0.5–1.0 (2)	Around 15 (2)	0.1–1.0 (2)	11	3
Dong Quang	0.5 (1)	0.5 (2)	0.5 (1)	5 (1)	1 (3)	8	1
Dong Ky	1.0 (2)	0.5 (2)	0.5 (1)	5 (1)	1 (3)	9	2
Phu khe	2.5 (5)	0.5 (2)	0.5 (1)	5 (1)	1 (3)	12	4

Notes: * Sub-districts have better facilities and more non-agricultural activities than other villages.
** Upcoming industrial district with good numbers of small hamlets, most of which have smal and tiny industrial units.
*** Growing industrial district.

Table 5.7: Usability of different facilities

Villages surveyed	Condition of various facilities (km)					
	Main road	Road condition	Mode of transportation	Electrification	Availability of electricity	Rank
Phuoc An	0.03	Good	Personal	Full	Regular	5
Zung B	1.5	Good	Personal	Partial	Regular	1
Ban	0.5	Good	Personal	Partial	Regular	2
Buon Phe	0.1	Good	Personal	Partial	Uncertain	3
Phuoc Hoa	0.5	Good	Personal	Full	Regular	3
Phroc Loe	0.3	Good	Personal	Full	Regular	4
13 Villages	0.5–2.0	Good	Personal	Full	Regular	3
Dong Quang	0.5	Very good	Personal	Full	Regular	4
Dong Ky	0.5	Very good	Personal	Full	Regular	4
Phu khe	0.5	Very good	Personal	Full	Regular	4

Notes: * Sub-districts have better facilities and more non-agricultural activities than other villages.
** Upcoming industrial district with good numbers of small hamlets, most of which have small and tiny industrial units.
*** Growing industrial district.

Table 5.8: ICT services used by villagers

Villages surveyed (Household, Population)	ICT services used by villagers					
	Postal	Telephone	Fax	Internet	Mobile	Rank
Phuoc An (3850, 19685)	Main	Main	Rare	Main	Main	1
Zung B (310, 1780)	Main	Occasional	Rare	Rare	Rare	4
Ban (217, 1294)	Main	Occasional	Rare	Rare	Rare	4
Buon Phe (225, 1194)	Main	Main	Rare	Occasional	Rare	3
Phuoc Hoa (665, 3789)	Main	Main	Rare	Occasional	Occasional	2
Phroc Loe (536, 2321)	Main	Main	Rare	Occasional	Rare	3
13 Villages (Household no. Max 270 and Min 88) (Population Max 1125 and Min 330)	Main	Main	Rare	Main	Occasional	1
Dong Quang	Main	Main	Rare	Main	Main	1
Dong Ky	Main	Main	Rare	Main	Main	1
Phu khe	Main	Main	Rare	Main	Main	1

has been made among types of services like postal (the traditional mode of communication) and mobile or Internet (the most modern modes of communications). We have imputed numbers for the extent of use of a service in the following way: 3 for main use, 2 for occasional use, and 1 for rare use of a type of ICT. Imputed values for all services have been added up to get the value for total extent of use of ICT for a particular village, and the villages were ranked accordingly.

Purpose of the Use of ICT Services

The survey also aimed at shedding light on the purposes for which the villagers accessed various ICT services. The purposes were broadly categorized as social contact, study/ education related, business related, and profession related, market related ones. In fact, there were other categories like health and medical related as well as other legal and administration related issues. Table 5.9 presents the categories for which responses were received. For the extent of use of ICT for a particular purpose, responses were sought in terms of 'main', 'occasional' and 'rare'. Again we have made a distinction of 'users' and 'non-users' (of MCTs) from the respondents of a village. The expectation has been a differentiable purpose of the use of ICT over the attributes like 'student', 'teacher', 'business man', 'traders', etc. The hypothesis we had in mind was that the business people would need more extensive use of ICTs. Hence, either they would be having their own arrangements or they would be the most extensive users of the MCT facilities.

From Table 5.9 it is not directly evident as to what are the predominating purposes of use of ICT services. Personal discussion, however, bring out the fact that growing business sector is the major users of the ICT services. Besides these, it is the student as community which is major user of Internet services.

We have imputed the value 3 for main use of a purpose, 2 for occasional use and 1 for rare use. The last column of Table 5.9 gives the linear addition of the values over the purposes for a village for both user and non-user respondents. These values are used to derive some attributed values to measure the 'difference in purpose'.

Association between ICT and Other Socio-economic Indicators

Table 5.10 has been prepared with the data from Tables 5.5 to 5.9, including the ranking of the villages in terms of 'ruralness' (Table 5.5), 'remoteness' (Table 5.6), accessibility of facilities (Table 5.7), ICT use (Table 5.8) and purpose value (Table 5.9). It raises a number of important questions such as: Is it the state of the economy that decides the extent of

Table 5.9: Purpose of ICT use by villagers

Village	Respondent	Social Contacts	Study/Education	Purpose Business	Profession	Market	Purpose value
Phuoc An	User	Main	Main	Main	Main	Main	15
	Non-user	Occasionally	-	Main	Occasionally	-	7
Zung B	User	Main	Main	Main	Main	Main	15
	Non-user	Main	-	Main	-	-	6
Ban	User	Main	-	Main	-	-	6
	Non-user	Main	-	-	-	-	3
Buon Phe	User	Main	-	Occasionally	-	-	5
	Non-user	Main		Occasionally			5
Phuoc Hoa	User	Main	-	Occasionally	-	-	5
	Non-user	Occasionally	-	-	-	-	5
Phuoc Loe	User	Main	-	Occasionally	-	-	5
	Non-user	Main	-	Main	-	-	6
Bac Giang	User	Main	Main	Main	Main	Main	15
(13 Vill)	Non-user	Occasionally	-	Main	-	-	5
Dong Quang	User	Main	Main	Main	Main	Main	15
	Non-user	Occasionally	-	-	-	-	2
Dong Ky	User	Main	Main	Main	Main	Main	15
	Non-user	Occasionally	-	-	-	-	2
Phu khe	User	Main	Main	Main	Main	Main	15
	Non-user	Occasionally	-	-	-	-	2

ICT use? Do the purposes of ICT use differ according to the state of the economy? If so, why are there users and non-users of MCT facilities in a given village?

We have tried to address the first two questions using Table 5.10, where we have ranks of villages in terms of ruralness, remoteness, accessibility and ICT use. We also have the difference in purpose value between users and non-users from the same villages calculated from Table 5.9. Various correlations among them have been tried. The results are presented in Table 5.11.

Table 5.10: Relative rural and remoteness of the villages

Villages	Ruralness	Remoteness in terms of civic amenities		ICT use	Difference in purpose value
		Distance	Accessibility		
Phuoc An	6	8	5	1	8
Zung B	1	3	1	4	9
Ban	1	2	2	4	3
Buon Phe	3	5	3	3	0
Phuoc Hoa	2	1	3	2	0
Phroc Loe	4	4	4	3	-1
13 Villages	5	6	3	1	10
Dong Quang	7	9	4	1	13
Dong Ky	7	7	4	1	13
Phu khe	7	5	4	1	13

Table 5.11: Relation between ICT use and various socio-economic indicators

Correlations between	Type of correlations	Correlation coefficient
ICT and ruralness	Rank correlation	(-) 0.89
ICT and remoteness	Rank correlation	(-)0.70
ICT and access	Rank correlation	(-) 0.77
Access and purpose	Rank and assigned value	0.21
Remote and purpose	Rank and assigned value	0.64
Rural and purpose	Rank and assigned value	0.68

All the three indicators, namely 'ruralness', 'remoteness' and accessibility, have negative correlations with ICT use. The high magnitude (0.89) of the negative correlation between ICT use and 'ruralness' indicates that ICT use is indeed dependent on the state of industrialization of the region. Although of lower magnitude, both remoteness and accessibility also point to the same conclusion—the closer to the infrastructure facilities and the better the accessibility to transport, electricity, etc, the more intensive the use of ICTs.

In the second set of correlations, the same set of rank values for socio-economic indicators is observed in relation to the purpose of ICT use (the gap between assigned value for users and non-users of MCTs over different purposes of uses).

All the three indicators show positive relations with the purpose of use. It means that the lower rank value of a village is associated with a lower gap value of the purpose of ICT use between users and non-users of MCT facilities. Likewise, the higher the rank value of a village (implying more rural and remote economy), the higher the gap value of the purpose of ICT use between users and non-users of MCT facilities. In other words, in comparatively better-industrialized areas, the purposes of ICT use do not differ much between users and non-users of MCTs, while it does so in more rural areas.

Profile of the Users and Non-users of the MCT

The questionnaire used for the survey sought elaborate information on demographic profiles of the families of users and non-users of MCT facilities. Part of this information is presented in Table 5.12 (for users) and 5.13 (for non-users). It is evident from Table 5.12 and 5.13 that users and non-users show certain distinctive features. Quality of data did not allow us to perform any precise statistical exercise. However, certain features are still readable.

First important factor appears to be the number of members of family in the ICT friendly age group. We have assumed it to be in the age group between 10 and 40. Older people in many cases are quite opposed to the advent of Internet. This was also observed during our field visit (see box).

Impact of MCTs: Social Indicators

The survey indicates that the right question to be asked so far impact of MCTs is concened, is whether MCTs could keep pace with the social development that has been taking place, and not how much they have contributed to the social development of the region. The MCTs have been actually burdened with expectations on contribution towards much desired social development of poor and backward areas.

Regarding relations between ICT and economic development, appropriate indicators have to be associative and not deterministic.

The Vietnam case shows that in areas where industrialization is at a nascent stage, but social developmental programmes are creating a new ICT-friendly generation having high literacy rate and little gender bias, MCTs have critical role to play for integrating the new generation with the rest of the world.

A comparison between Table 5.12 and 5.13 for the column 'age group' shows that non-users families have smaller number of members in the ICT friendly age group. Again on an average 60% of the user's family has about two school-going children and 30% has at least 1 member doing higher education (Table 5.12).

In comparison, the figures for non-user families are 30% and 5% respectively.

Table 5.12: User's profile (percentage of respondent families)

Villages surveyed	Family size		Age group 10-20		Age group 20-40		School going		Higher education		Earning member	
	=< 5	>5	=< 2	>2	=<2	>2	=<2	>2	=1	>1	= 1	> 1
Phuoc An	35	65	20	25	40	30	60	30	30	-	20	80
Zung B	35	65	20	25	30	30	60	-	5	-	20	80
Ban	35	65	20	25	30	30	60	-	5	-	40	60
Buon Phe	20	80	20	25	20	30	60	30	10	-	20	80
Phuoc Hoa	20	80	20	25	20	30	60	30	10	-	20	80
Phroc Loe	20	80	20	25	20	30	60	30	10	-	20	80
Bac Giang(13 Vill)	50	50	20	25	40	40	70	-	40	-	20	80
Dong Quang	50	50	20	25	40	50	90	-	40	-	20	80
Dong Ky	50	50	20	25	40	50	90	-	40	-	20	80
Phu khe	50	50	20	25	40	50	90	-	40	-	20	80

Table 5.13: Non-user's profile (percentage of respondent families)

Villages surveyed	Family size		Age group 10-20		Age group 20-40		School going		Higher education		Earning member	
	=< 5	>5	=< 2	>2	=<2	>2	=<2	>2	=1	>1	= 1	> 1
Phuoc An	20	80	20	-	20	10	30	-	5	-	20	80
Zung B	20	80	20	10	20	10	30	-	5	-	20	60
Ban	10	90	20	10	20	10	30	-	5	-	20	80
Buon Phe	20	80	20	20	20	20	30	-	-	-	20	80
Phuoc Hoa	20	80	20	20	20	20	30	-	-	-	20	80
Phuoc Loe	20	80	20	20	20	20	30	-	5	-	20	80
Bac Giang(13 Vill)	30	70	30	-	20	30	80	-	20	-	50	50
Dong Quang	15	85	20	-	20	10	30	-	-	-	50	50
Dong Ky	15	85	20	-	20	10	30	-	-	-	50	50
Phu khe	15	85	20	-	20	10	30	-	-	-	50	50

What is not evident from the Tables but surfaced during the field visits and interviews with MCT personnel is that, in relatively industrialized areas, many business people are also non-users of MCT services. In fact, school children constitute the main users of MCTs, irrespective of geographical area or economic status. This appears to be a direct fruit of the widespread literacy programme launched by the government, which has attained nearly 100% school attendance.

Survey Insights

Survey of users and non-users of MCT services reinforces the broad understanding of relations between ICT and economic and social development. The results have important implications on the indicators for evaluation of impacts of MCTs.

> **Ms. Huong: Desirous to be a fashion designer**
>
> After Mr. Mien we met Ms. Huong a student of 8th standard. Only child of farmer parents, she wants to be a fashion designer. At her age she is matured enough to decide about her career. She visits the same MCT, where we met Mr. Mien, quite often and looks for sites related to fashion designing to update herself about the trends. She is aware that the trade is not well developed in Vietnam but has potentiality.

The survey has juxtaposed the relative economic and social status of the villages and has argued for direct correlations between economic status and the use of MCT.

The Vietnam economy is moving very fast towards industrialization as conscious policy decision through restructuring of the economy. Again, as brought out by the survey, the upcoming new generation are growing up with

Internet Vitiates the Young Mind

The ground floor of the two-storied building of the MCT at Bac Ninh has a reading room for the library and newspaper. The first person we met at the entrance was an elderly man, Mr. Mien. He was reading a newspaper when we drew his attention. He took no time to flare up the moment the issue of availability of Internet services came up. Highly critical of MCT for providing access to Internet, he was unhappy for the kind of ill effect it was casting on the society in general and on the young impressionable mind in particular. Mr. Mien is a Chemistry teacher in a high school. When asked about any positive effect he expressed his scepticism, since there was no control either on the technology or on the content.

MCT at Bac Ninh

high information orientation and ICT familiarity. This is a direct consequence of the educational policy followed by the government. This upcoming generation will match the changing economic status that is getting ready for lift-off. The MCTs in Vietnam are actually catalyzing the process of matching the two. If not through any other indicators, the most noteworthy impact of MCTs is reflected in the government policies to set up cultural points (with Internet accessibility) in every commune of Vietnam.

Ms. Que: A Budding Litterateur

Dreamy eyed Ms. Que is a student of class IX. We almost had to bang the table to draw her attention. Extremely shy, she told us about her passion for literature. She looks for sites on literature. Not much is available in the library near her village. She wants to know more about world literature. Do you write poetry or stories? Ms. Que sunk her head further down and in her almost inaudible soft voice said something. We could not make out if it was 'yes' or 'no'.

Cultural Points and Related Issues

In addition to MCTs we had the opportunities to visit two cultural points. The cultural point in Vietnam is an interesting concept. These are managed by communes—the lowest administrative unit constituted of people's representatives.

A commune is typically consisted of 8–10 villages. Originally conceptualized as a centre of common facilities for cultural activities for the villages under the commune, VNPT has extended the MCT concept to the commune level by establishing telecentres at the cultural points. There are about 8000 communes in 64 provinces of Vietnam. The programme of establishment of telecentres in 'cultural point' was initiated in 2003. By that time VNPT had already derived experience of establishing and running MCTs in four places. By 2005, about 7000 cultural points were established in different communes across the country. In some cases, as in two MCT project areas of Bac Ninh and Bac Giang cultural point have been established even at village levels. The VNPT has a target of covering all the communes under cultural point programme by the end of the current year, and also gradually extending the facility at the village level. To begin with a cultural point is provided with facilities like library, newspaper, telephone, postal services, and also Internet access. According to VNPT officials it is a scaled down concept of MCT. So a cultural point, instead of broadband ASDL, has a dial-up connection in low-end computers. As for the investment, telephone lines and Internet connections are provided by VNPT. The cost of telephone lines in remote areas may go up to US$ 600. The VNPT access the Universal Service Fund created from fees collected from telecom operators. So far equipping the cultural point is concerned, the postal services are arranged by VNPT. Books and newspaper are mostly arranged and collected as gifts from individuals and organizations. The cultural point is managed by the respective commune, and generally manned by one staff selected by the commune from the villages. Basic concept remaining the same, actual management of the cultural point depends on the policies of the respective communes. Two typical cultural point are profiled below.

Cultural Point at Duong Son Village Under Tam Son Commune in Tu Son District

Established in 2004, the building for the cultural point was given by the commune. TheICT equipment was provided by VNPT at Bac Nihn. The cultural point has two primary schools and a secondary school in the vicinity. The commune has large number of small enterprises making wooden furniture, wood processing, and iron and steel works, etc. It has also substantial horticultural products exported to Hanoi, the capital city of Vietnam. As expected the teledensity of the district Tu Son is way above the national average.

Cultural point at Tam Son

The cultural point has a library, two computer terminals with dial-up Internet connections, postal services and a stage for cultural performance.

In a normal day there are about 10–15 users of the ICT facilities. As reported by the operator, telephone users are essentially elderly people and business personnel, whereas Internet is generally used by younger people, mainly school children. The facilities are available for 10 hours a day, from 10 am to 7 pm, with half an hour lunch break in between.

The cultural point is run by one employee selected by the commune. The operator is paid US$ 14 per month, of which US$ 6 is paid by VNPT for postal services provided, another US$ 6 is paid by the commune, and the rest is earned as 10% commission on the revenue earned by the cultural point.

Cultural Point at Xuan Phu Commune in Bac Giang P&T

Smaller in size, the cultural point at Xuan Phu has a little less impressive look than the one at Tam Son. The building of the cultural point was donated by Bac Giang P&T. For a total population of 9000, the commune has one secondary and one military school.

Children at a cultural point

The economic activities are not as diversified in Xuan Phu as in Tam Son, but the cultural point provides similar facilities such as telephone, two computers with dial-up connections, postal services and a library set-up with donations from individuals and organizations.

The cultural point is managed by the commune with one employee selected from the local people. The employee gets about US$ 20 per month as remuneration. The Bac Giang P&T pay the difference, if any, between cost and revenue.

Army school students constitute about 50% of the telephony users. Internet facilities are generally used by school children. Business units have their own arrangements and do not use the cultural point facilities.

Sustainability and Replicability: The Emergence of a Vietnam Model

As admitted by the President of PTIT, the cultural points in Vietnam are direct offshoot of the MCT concept. It is felt that cultural points, indeed, provide a model of information service network for universal accessibility in developing countries. They also propose a new dimension in sustainability, replicability and partnership for the MCT project.

The Vietnam Model

At the core of this network are the MCTs, providing high-end information services, surrounded by satellite information centres at community level (suitable aggregation of villages, depending on the logistics) which provide lower-end information services. The veracity of the model being conditional on the social and economic milieu within which it has to function, the Vietnam model will accordingly be constructed in line with the social and economic backdrop of Vietnam.

It is to be remembered that we are talking about an economy that is at an early stage of transition to an industrial economy. Also to be noted that the Vietnamese economy is not diversified enough; private enterprises are a new development; market for information is in its nascent stage; and use of ICT is limited mainly to basic services. At the same time the economy is poised for a high rate of economic growth, and has upcoming ICT and information savvy highly literate new generation.

Such an economy needs to be developed on the one hand for high-end information services to match the future high-growth economy and on the other hand for initiation of the common people to acquaint with the power and potential of information and ICT. Both these roles have to be performed simultaneously to avoid any lopsided development of information market and creation of a new generation of information haves ant have-nots. Scarcity of resource that generally plagues a developing economy, together with the capital cost associated with MCTs, Vietnam cannot undertake both the roles concurrently. The cultural point, described as a scale-down low cost version of MCTs, complements MCTs by assuming the supporting role.

There are various possibilities of organizational and logistic structure that would eventually link both MCTs and cultural points. Ideally it can be visualized that MCTs, being technologically better equipped, will conceptualize, design and develop various application modules and required connectivity, whereas cultural points will operate as the access points to information, subject to shaping of the economies around them, and gradually evolve into MCTs.

Sustainability and Related Issues

The model of complementarities between MCT and cultural points can provide answers to many questions raised in the MCT pilot project.

As far as sustainability is concerned, Table 5.3 has shown that the MCTs are not financially sustainable. If we make a distinction between private rate of return (in this case the rate of return to MCTs) and social rate of return to investment, it is obvious that social rate of return is much higher than the rate of return to MCTs. High social rate of return is indicated by the increasing number of users of MCT services, particularly by the younger generations. The information intensity of this new generation and the use of ICT by them will be at much higher level in future, and shall bring in the necessary mass for the sustainability of MCTs. Such indications are already noticeable at cultural points level, where people in large number are being introduced to ICTs and gradually becoming a new information-intensive society. In other words, the core ideas of MCTs are being sustained through cultural points'.

Another indication of sustainability is the significant investment in cultural points sparked off by the idea of MCTs. The basic lesson is that the MCT tenet of universal access to ICT is not wholly inflexible and could, in fact, co-exist with various sustainability models, according to the conditions specific to the concerned country. In the case of Vietnam, MCTs have proliferated in the form of cultural points. Other alternatives, (equally or more sustainable), could certainly be found and explored in different contexts.

Observations

The economy of Vietnam is on the take-off track. At least in the two provinces where MCTs are located, there is proliferation of new small enterprises. Many of them have their own websites and aspire to operate globally. Spread of education along with extensive industrial development programmes has created new economic opportunities. Use of ICT is also gearing up both for business and professional use and also by the younger generations.

When compared with the cases of Timbuctu, Bhutan and Honduras, it is clear that the economy of villages around the MCTs in Vietnam is different in diversity and dynamics. The government initiative to make ICT services accessible to rural and remote areas enabled the people to capitalize on the new opportunities. That does not mean that the spread of economic development which is being witnessed in the rural areas of Vietnam is the result of the access to ICT services. What Vietnam has achieved is coupling the access to ICT services with the developmental programmes that created new opportunities for individual initiatives. In case of Honduras, lack of such opportunities has wasted the advantage of high rates of literacy. On the other hand, Bhutan is still a stage behind but in the process of gaining advantage of literacy and availability of economic opportunities. The case of Timbuctu remained an exemplary case of marginal economy.

6

MCTs in Nicaragua

An Alternative Mode of Access

Introduction

The Ministry of Public Health in Nicaragua has created the local integrated health systems SILAIS in order to make health related information and expertise available in remote areas. This has been made possible by multi-agencies initiatives. The International Telecommunication Union (ITU), Telecommunication Regulatory Body (TELCOR) and the Ministry of Public Health (MINSA) joined together in the efforts of establishing a Telehealth MCT Pilot Project based on data communication system, instead of a voice-oriented telecommunication network to transmit information among the SILAIS of Chinandega and MINSA, Managua. The main objective of this project was to harmonize and reinforce the vigilance systems of the public health and epidemiology as well as the disaster prevention and management.

Under the initiative of the ITU Central American Office, a pilot project was established in order to set-up a data network located in one of the most vulnerable areas in the north-west part of the country. Under this initiative, ITU, MINSA and TELCOR have a working network in seven small villages and the network has been expanded to more than 12 villages under a regular project.

The initial network was equipped with seven packet radio stations, including 1 repeater. The stations are located in the Epidemiology Department of MINSA in Managua, and in the SILAIS, Chinandega. The station in Chinandega is located in the village Chinandega, and also in the health centre of Chinandega, Corinto, El Viejo and Villanueva. The repeater station is located in the health centre of San Jose de Cusmapa. The actual network is equipped with 12 stations and the bandwidth has been upgraded to handle transmission rate up to 72 kbps.

Each packet radio station is equipped with the following:

- 1 PC
- 1 TNC Kantronics KPC 9612 Plus
- 1 Radio transceptor ALINCO DR-605T Dualband
- 1 Power supply ASTRON RS-20M de 15 DCV y 25 Amps.
- 1 Directional/omni-directional VHF/UVF Antenna

Figure 6.1 shows as to how each packet radio station is configured in the network

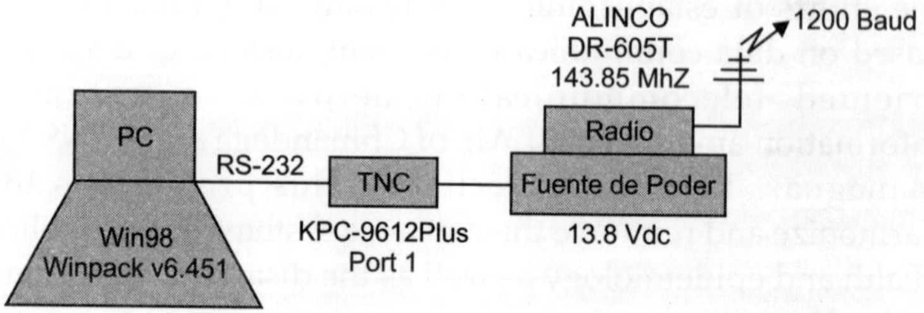

Fig. 6.1: Configuration packet radio station

Locations of the project and villages where the stations are installed are shown in the following map (Fig. 6.2).

The MCT network is managed by MINSA and has a dual purpose to carry out the administrative part of the public health mainly in the area of epidemiology and also to augment disaster management.

Fig. 6.2: Location of project and stations

Figures 6.3 and 6.4 show the nature of the network configured to centralize the information in the main office of the Ministry of Public Health of Nicaragua where the specialized staffs reside. From the technical point of view, TCPIP protocol is used on the top of packet radio. Therefore, the system is ready to be interfaced with Internet in a transparent way. In this model, all typical modes such as SMTP and FTP are used mainly on the file-transfer activities.

Ministry of Public Health MINSA and ITU

The mission of MINSA is to ensure that the population has access to health services which respond to their real and perceived needs, and that the health system emphasizes

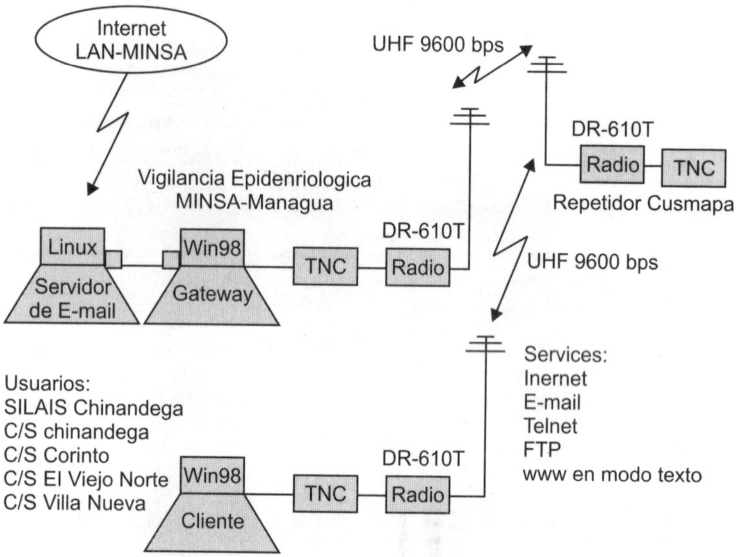

Fig. 6.3: Packet radio network using TCP/IP

health promotion and prevention of disease through an integrated and humane approach. The major challenges that the Ministry of Health must address in order to fulfill its mission and advance the process of institutional reform are to (i) incorporate new modalities of organization and administration, (ii) adopt new financing alternatives, modernize hospitals, (iii) promote the protection of investments in infrastructure and equipment, (iv)establish and provide a basic package of essential services, (v) prioritize high-risk areas and groups, (vi) promote health and prevent diseases, (vii) achieve efficiency in the use of resources, and (viii) improve management control systems. Table 6.1 presents the human resources distribution in SILAIS at Chinandega and Managna.

ICT Application to the Development

The cost involved in establishing reasonably functioning network for tele-medicine makes it beyond the reach of the

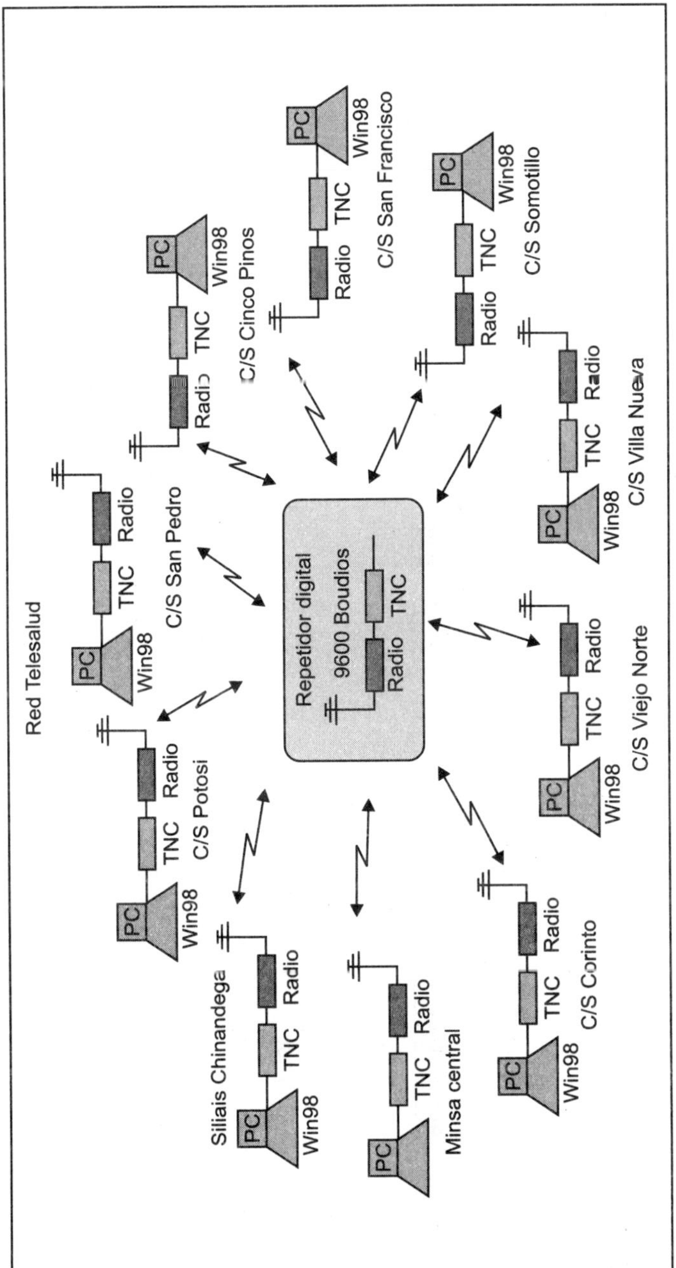

Fig. 6.4: Telehealth network in 10 villages

Table 6.1: Ministry of Public Health Personnel in SILAIS at Chinandega and Managua

	Human Resource Distribution in SILAIS Chinandega and Managua							
SILAIS at	**Administrators**	**Nurse asst**	**Nurses**	**Specl Doctors**	**General Doctors**	**Odontologists**	**Technicians**	**Total**
Chinandega	539	355	153	88	114	27	358	1,634
Managua	3,047	1,058	461	403	271	56	1,550	6,846
Total	3,586	1,413	614	491	385	83	1,908	8,480

rural population in developing countries. Networks with a wideband capability in order to transport electronic images imply a high operation and maintenance cost. But it is not only the cost of the telecommunication infrastructure which counts, the cost of equipment and their operation and maintenance at the user end is also equally high.

Telehealth, on the other hand, may be the first step for a developing country to establish a telecommunication infrastructure with a low maintenance and operation cost as well as a simple technology adapted from other well-developed applications. Radio equipment on the VHF and UHF bands designed for voice applications can be easily converted to digital transmission keeping prices under a low range. Technologies such as packet radio, using TCPIP or even X.25 protocols are being tested and successfully applied to rural areas in Central America.

The network established by MINSA with the technical assistance of ITU has provided a roadway to transport all the data of the Epidemiology Programme of Nicaragua. The software developed by the Institution carries all the necessary information required by the program. The bandwidth leftover after the Epidemiology application is used for disaster relief and management. At present ITU is upgrading the bandwidth to provide basic Internet services to the people, in general, in the villages and hamlets where the network has been established.

Pilot Project and Actual Project

Four years ago, MINSA had established a comprehensive radio network for voice communications with the main purpose of reaching the rural health centers established in a large number of remote villages having no telecommunication services. The establishment of the voice network was a big step in order to establish some type of telecommunication for administrative purposes and medical emergencies.

Soon the Epidemiology Department of MINSA started collecting data from the villages by means of reading out numbers and statistics as well as the data on current state of the public health in the countryside.

Nicaragua as part of Central America is prone to several hurricanes and natural disasters. The network is the only means of communication for the disaster-affected areas.

The voice application was an error-prone media to transmit accurate information. The ITU technical assistance programme started applying concepts and ideas of a "light data telecommunication network (LTN) as a pilot project under the Valetta Action Plan (VAP) of the Development Bureau BDT of ITU. The LTN was using the same infrastructure and introduced the terminal equipment composed of PC and radio modems to establish a working network which was to be installed, operated and maintained by the local people.

The pilot project had been working for the past four years, and a new radio equipment having a larger bandwidth, along with a newer version of radio modems are now providing a 72 kbps network with access to Internet and capable of transmitting graphics. Six new stations are being piloted together with the old ones and the entire network is being upgraded. As for the terminal equipment, refurbished PC equipment from the central offices of ITU is being shipped to fill the needs of these remote locations.

Applications

The LTN established by the project has two clear areas of applications: (i) Telehealth and (ii) Disaster prevention relief and management. The most frequent application is the one oriented to telehealth. Daily consultation between rural health centres and the MINSA headquarters (located in the capital city of Managua) is operational. The MINSA has access to a medium size group of specialists associated with public hospitals which are able to solve or help to solve daily health situations or to participate in the decision making of transporting patients to better-equipped health centre. The network has enabled MINSA for early detection of possible epidemic, creating awareness regarding spread of diseases like cholera and also for control and prevention of epidemics.

During the natural disaster such as the one caused by hurricane, the LTN has been proved to be the only media able to reach the affected rural population. The relief agencies were the users of the relaying communication means provided by this project.

Profile of the Villages Served by the Network

The profiles of villages and health centres under SILAI in Chinandega are presented in Table 6.2.

These are the health centres to be benefited by the telemedicine information network project. Except a few villages (health centres) around Chinandega, other health centres are very far off, economically poorer and smaller in size. It is to be noted that even the poor villages have significantly high literacy.

Table 6.3 gives an idea of ruralness of the villages. In terms of economic profiles, villages range mainly from agriculture to traditional household industries, to cattle breeding or fishing economies. Village San Juan de Cinco Pinos has large number of SMEs and, therefore, can be called less rural as compared to other villages.

Table 6.4 depicts the relative remoteness of the villages/ health centres surveyed.

The village San Juan de Cinco Pinos, which has high dependence on SMEs, is also the remotest in terms of all the parameters.

The quality of infrastructural facilities in the villages are presented in Table 6.5.

Table 6.2: Profile of the villages

Village/health centre	Distance from MCT (km)	No. of household	Total population	Literacy (%)	General Economic Condition
Chinandega	0	81100	441308	80	Average
Chinandega Health Center	0	32221	153534	75	Average
El ViejoHealth Center	0	17865	92765	78	Average
VillanuevaHealth Center	0	5100	29165	84	Average
San Pedro del NorteHealth Center	120	1020	4306	80	Poor
CusmapaHealth Center	0	1270	6340	-	Poor
San Juan de Cinco PinosHealth Center	0	1458	6772	83.5	poor
Corinto Health Center	0	4100	21000	75	Average

Table 6.3: Relative ruralness of the villages

Village/health centre	Sectoral contribution (%)				
	Agriculture	Minerals	H'hold Industry	SMEs	Other
Chinandega	32	23	45	-	-
Chinandega health centre	32	23	45	-	-
El Viejohealth centre	82		7	1	8
Villanuevahealth centre	61	7	5	6	20
San Pedro del Nortehealth centre	95	-	-	-	5
Cusmapahealth centre	45	-	-	5	50 Cattle breeding
San Juan de Cinco Pinoshealth centre	12	-	-	80	8
Corinto health center	-	-	-	10	90 Fishing

Table 6.4: Relative remoteness of the villages

Village/health centre	Distance of the nearest market (km)	Distance of the nearest hospital (km)	Distance of the nearest higher education centre (km)	Distance of the nearest post office (km)
Chinandega	2	0.5	2.5	3
Chinandega health centre	2	0.5	2.5	3
El Viejohealth centre	1	6	0.5	0.5
Villanuevahealth centre	18	8	2	1.5
San Pedro del Nortehealth centre	30	120	35	40
Cusmapahealth centre	35	36	39	36
San Juan de Cinco Pinoshealth centre	33	112	48	33
Corinto health centre	1.8	8	2	1.5

Table 6.5: Relative infrastructure facilities in the villages

Village/health centre	Road network	Main modes of transport	Electrification	Availability of electricity
Chinandega	Good	Public/own	FullRegular	
El Viejo	Bad	Public/own	Partial	Regular
Villanueva	Bad	Public/own	Partial	Regular
San Pedro del Norte	Bad	PublicPartial	Regular	
Cusmapa	Bad	PublicPartial	Uncertain	
San Juan de Cinco Pinos	Bad	PublicPartial	Regular	
Corinto	Bad	Public/own	Partial	Uncertain

The overall condition of general infrastructural facilities indicates the general economic backwardness of the villages.

Table 6.6 gives the use pattern of ICT in the villages/ health centre studied. It is evident from Table 6.6 that the availability of ICT services is skeletal in the villages.

Table 6.6: ICT use pattern of the villages

Village/ Health Center	Postal service	Phone	Telefax	Internet	Mobile
Chinandega	Occasional	Main	Occasional	Occasional	Main
El Viejo	Occasional	Main	Rare	Rare	Main
Villanueva	Occasional	Main	Rare	Rare	Main
San Pedro del Norte					Main
Cusmapa	-	Main	-	-	-
San Juan de Cinco Pinos		Main	Rare	Occasional	
Corinto	Occasional	Main	Rare	Rare	Main

Present Status

The Health Care Centre of Nicaragua is an efficient data point to access information. These centres are equipped with a data terminal which is able to handle heavier use, and the LTN has enough bandwidth to support a small size LAN to provide services to the communities besides its use in the Epidemiology Department of the Ministry of Public Health. A proposal to MINSA is on the way to provide Internet access to the population of the small villages and to make a case of economic self-sustainability.

Observation on MCTs in Nicaragua

Nicaragua presents an alternative model for the use of ICT for social benefits of the people in rural and remote areas. Unlike the four cases discussed earlier, here ICT services are geared to a particular social cause, such as public health and disaster management. This is an answer to the dilemma of orienting access to ICT services as to whether it is to be individual based or community based. The present study has observed that a rural community with underdeveloped social and economic infrastructure and rare economic opportunities can be better served by community oriented ICT services as opposed to providing services targeting only the individuals. Literacy rate being high, people would be able to use the information that concerns health and natural calamity. The same mode can be used in the case of Honduras and Bhutan. In case of Timbuctu, the level of intervention has to be more direct.

7

MCTs in Tanzania

Serving the Dispossessed

Introduction

The Ngara MCT Network Project supported by ITU, Tanzania Commission of Science and Technology (COSTECH), the United Nations Educational, Scientific and Cultural Organisation (UNESCO), the United Nations High Commission for Refugees (UNHCR) and the Tanzania Communication Regulatory Authority (TCRA), is located at three sites, namely K9, Lukole Camp A and the Ngara Town Community Centre. Overall, the telecentres' mission is to bring ICT to the community and enable this remote population to access electronic information and build capacity to participate more actively in socio-cultural and economic development. This is particularly pertinent to the geographically isolated populations as it empowers them to take part in the matters that affect their lives.

The Resolution 37 of the Plenipotentiary Conference of ITU held in Kyoto in 1994 called for "continued efforts towards the application of the relevant United Nations (UN) resolutions relating to assistance to refugees...". The UN High Commissioner for Refugees stressed the importance of launching educational programmes for refugees using information technologies, etc. The Ngara Multipurpose Community Telecentre Network Project in Tanzania was initiated on the above lines in 2002 and commenced operation towards the end of 2003.

Budget

A total budget of US$ 123,250 was estimated for the project to cover the first two years expenditure, which was to be funded by ITU and UNESCO. The budget included the cost of purchasing of equipment and materials and meeting the initial administrative costs in first two years. UNHCR provided the building and electricity for K9 and Lukole centres.

The charges for E-mail and Internet at Ngara MCT are T. Shillings 1,000 and 500 for one hour and half an hour, respectively.

In terms of location, the Project could not have been set in a more remote site as the region has the lowest per capita Gross Domestic Product(GDP) as well as the lowest urbanization level in Mainland Tanzania.

Ngara District

Ngara District with a population of 334,939 is one of the six administrative districts of Kagera Region. There are four divisions with 49,082 households and an average population of 6.8 per household. The four divisions (with their population given in brackets) are Rusumo (123,119), Rulenge (20,497), Kabanga (18,038) and Ngara Town (15,687). Ngara district belongs to the Highland Economic Zone together with Muleba, Karagwe and Muleba Rural districts. The district has 442,800 acres of arable land of which only 72,000 acres are used. The economy is mainly based on subsistence farming. Banana and highland rice are the main agricultural products from the region. Forests cover is 2,522 sq km or 57% of the whole district's area of 4,428 sq km.

There are four primary schools, five secondary schools, two hospitals and two dispensaries in the town. In July 2005, the town was connected to the national power grid. A new secondary school is under construction near Shunga Mountain (the highest point in Kagera region), between Ngara and Rusumo townships. Telecommunication services became available in 2000.

K 9

K9, located 17 km away from Ngara town and 9 km from Lukole refugee camps, is the base of a number of organizations which work with and in the refugee camps and has a population of approximately 600. Such organizations include the Norwegian People's Aid (NPA), Atlas Logistics, Concern International, Jesuit Refugee Services as well as the Tanzania Peoples' Defence Forces (TPDF) and the Ministry of Home Affairs. All these organizations have their offices and residential quarters at the base. The site also has a girls' secondary school with about 200 pupils and 25 teachers. The NPA has two generators which run alternately throughout the day, mainly to power the refrigeration unit for the storage of vaccines.

The main development since the introduction of the MCT towards the end of 2003, has been the extension of its network to the girls' secondary school's library. Between January 2004 and October 2005, 52 community members had successfully attended basic computer sensitization courses run by the Network Manager. The Manager is assisted by a volunteer in opening and closing the centre when he is at the other network points. There is no charge for e-mail and Internet to members but the introduction of a small fee is under serious consideration.

Lukole Camps

There are two refugee camps: Lukole A and Lukole B, separated by a two kilometre long valley with an estimated population of 50,000 and 45,000 respectively. There are 13 primary schools in the camps, each with about 200 pupils and 20 teachers. There is no secondary school. The MCT planned to follow the practices of Schoolnet of South Africa in order to serve the educational needs of the post-primary school students. Among the residents, there are 3,100 people with secondary school education and 140 with post secondary education. This is the group that has been most active in the use of the centre as well as in articulating the need to expand the centre and to provide more educational content. The project document had noted, "an MCT with educational facilities and appropriate content can greatly contribute to the educational process of children and teachers".

Ngara Telecentre

The Ngara telecentre is located in a spacious room at the Town Community Centre which is surrounded by a number of public services and Non-Government Organizations (NGO) including the Tanzania Red Cross, Green Hope Organization – a youth health counselling centre, as well as an Assemblies of God Church and a Mosque within a stone's throw distance. Other public services like the central market, post office, Tanzania Electricity Company, National Microfinance Bank, hospitals, UN agencies offices and the district administrative offices are found within walking distance of the telecentre.

The Ngara telecentre has great potential to provide additional services such as helping the teachers to design school programmes. Other community members may learn designing of business cards, wedding cards for social parties and other ceremonies.

Services and Users

E-mail services and the introductory computer courses are the two popular services offered by the MCT. As pointed out by most of the respondents, the time allocated to each registered member (1 hour per week broken into 2 slots of 30 minutes each) is not enough. Most of the non-users, the majority of who are office goers, cannot make use of this facility because the centre is already closed by the time they are free from their own office work. Refugees who do not have any regular income need not pay for the use of e-mail facility.

The MCT is powered by a single NPA generator which is only switched on for 3 to 5 hours a day (Monday to Friday) when the medical team from K9 works at the camp's hospital. The Very Small Aperture Terminal (VSAT) satellite dish was installed in July 2005.

On an average the centre had 278 registered e-mail users—on an average 25 users a day. The users have a demand for "mobile library" software so that its members could access information sources for professional and educational advancement.

38 out of the 46 non-user respondents pointed out "lack of familiarity with ICT" and "inconvenient timing" as the reasons for not using the facilities. Inadequate space is also considered as a constraint on the expansion of activities of MCT. Again 36 out of 54 respondents use Internet as their main mode of communication.

Project Highlights

The main challenges to Ngara and Lukole telecentres are to maintain and sustain the interest generated by them among the local populace. Ngara faced the additional challenge of exploring ways and means of becoming financially self-sustaining after the initial two years, during which the financing was being provided by donor agencies. Other services, which became quickly popular, included CD burning, secretarial service, and telephone and photo-copying service. The latter two services were found to be quite costly in town when compared to Dar es Salaam prices.

Lack of reliable transport and the absence of a training assistant were pointed out as other problems which limit the MCT from promoting and expanding its services to the existing and potential users in town and in the other administrative divisions of the district.

Assessment of Impact: Views from Users and Non-users

Following are the views of the local people on how to enhance the effective reach of MCT, as expressed during the interviews:

- There is a need for more publicity to the local community, either through local radio or public notice boards.
- The MCT could sell laptops/PC accessories like mouse, flash disks, etc through the MCT.
- Provide network connections to plug in laptops.
- Some advertisement would be goodfor revenue generation.
- Accessing information via Internet may be too expensive for farmers—concessional pricing could be an option.
- Accessories like printers could be added.
- New and faster computers are needed.
- More users could be trained on the services and its advantages, as users and potential users need more ICT sensitization.
- MCT's could increase service hours and should consider opening during weekends and after office hours when most employees return home from work.

Non-users reasons for not using the facility are as follows:

- Lack of training in ICT.
- Not being informed about the MCT and its programmes.

- Not being familiar with the English language.
- The centre is closed when one comes back from work (like, in case of a teacher).
- Working space is narrow and time allocated for each member is inadequate.
- There is no privacy as other may read what an user is writing.

General Observations

(i) The Ngara-based MCT network in a refugee environment has taken off well. The MCT at Lukole camp in particular, appears to have achieved one of its main objectives of serving as a vehicle for social integration amongst the refugees. Programmes and activities are needed to sustain and nurture the current enthusiasm. This can be achieved by introducing education-based programmes and also by making the MCT premises more attractive in terms of facilities as well as work environment. With the right equipment and guidance, the refugees could become their own resource persons.

(ii) Reliance on refugee volunteers to oversee the daily operations at the Lukole MCT appears to be working well. There is, however, a need to consider financial incentives to the managers for their own sustenance.

(iii) The Ngara MCT is currently working on creating a Local Content chapter for the project by adding to its current services the provision of relevant local news sourced from both local and international sources and by documenting local history and skills.

The profiles of the villages studied are given in Table 7.1.

Table 7.1: Village profile

Village	Distance from MCT	No. of household	Total population	Literacy (%)	General economic condition
K9	0 km		600	90	Refugee camp
Ngara	0 km	3395	15687	90	Poor
Lukole	0 km	12000	95000	90	Refugee camp

It is evident from the Table that the villages are poor with high literacy. Lukole is a huge refugee camp and suffers from the crisis of basic facilities related to health and hygiene.

Table 7.2 presents the rurallness of the economy on the basis of the selected economic indicators.

Table 7.2: Economy Ruralness

Village	Sectoral contribution				
	AGR.	Minerals	H'hold industry	SMEs	Other
K9	Nil	Nil	Nil	Nil	Refugee camps
Ngara	Mainly	Nil	Nil	Nil	
Lukole	Nil	Nil	Nil	Nil	Refugee camps

Ngara is a regular settled village and is exclusively dependent on agriculture. The rest are refugee camps and many households do not have any source of regular income. Table 7.3 shows the remoteness of the villages.

Table 7.3: Remoteness of the villages

Village	Distance of the nearest market (in km.)	Distance of the nearest hospital (in km.)	Distance of the nearest higher education centre (in km.)	Distance of the nearest post office (in km.)
K9	0	0	0	0
Ngara	0	0	300	0
Lukole	28	Camp hospital	0	0

Ngara has the facilities, other than higher education centre, all in the town itself. Others are refugee camps and most of the services are provided by the various international agencies and NGOs.

Table 7.4 presents information about the infrastructural facilities of the villages.

Table 7.4: Infrastructure

Village	Road network	Main modes	Electrification	Availability of electricity
K9	Good	Public	Nil	NA
Ngara	Very good	Public	Partial	Uncertain
Lukole	Bad	Public	Nil	NA

The refugee camps do not have electricity, whereas Ngara has partial electrification with uncertain availability.

The pattern of ICT use of the villages is given in Table 7.5.

Table 7.5: ICT use pattern

Village	Postal service	Telephone	Telefax	Internet	Mobile
K9	Occasional	Main	Rare	Main	Nil
Ngara	Occasional	Main	Rare	Main	Nil
Lukole	Occasional	Main	Rare	Main	Nil

Telephone and Internet services are the main ICT services accessed by the people in the refugee camps as well as villagers in Ngara.

Users and Non-users of the ICT Services

The survey covered the respondents from these villages as shown in Table 6.

Table 7.6: Number of user and non-user of MCT services surveyed

Name of village	User	Non-user
K9	13	Nil
Ngara	33	17
Lukole	54	46

Table 7.7 gives the economic profiles of the villages.

Table 7.7: Livelihood of the users and non-users

Main source of earning	Types	Farming	Business	Service
K9	User	Nil	Nil	13
	Non-user	Nil	Nil	
Ngara	User	3	1	14
	Non-user	2	7	3
Lukole	User	2	3	43
	Non-user	5	9	32

It is observed that the users of ICT services are mainly from the services sector. In the refugee camps petty business people also use ICTs. Table 7.8 explores the use pattern further for ICT friendly age group in the families surveyed.

Table 7.8: Number of families having number of members in the ICT friendly age group (15–40 years)

Villages	Types	One	Two	Three	Four	Five	Six and more
K9	User	1	7	1			
	Non-user						
Ngara	User	9	9	2	2	1	1
	Non-user	1	7	1	1	1	1
Lukole	User	13	28	2	3	1	0
	Non-user	12	19	1	2	0	1

The demographic features of the family are more or less the same for Ngara and refugee camps, and also between users and non-users in these settlements.

Table 7.9 shows number of families having number of school going children, where as Table 7.10 gives the same for children going for higher education.

Numbers of school going children do not explain the user and non-user distinction. It is, therefore, more governed by the general economic conditions of the families.

Table 7.9: Number of families having school going children

Villages	Types	One	Two	Three	Four	Five and more
K9	User	2	3			
	Non-user					
Ngara	User	3	4	3	3	
	Non-user	5	-	2	3	3
Lukole	User	10	9	7	6	4
	Non-user	8	16	5	7	4

Table 7.10: Number of families having children going for higher education

Villages	Types	One	Two	Three
K9	User			
	Non-user			
Ngara	User	4	4	
	Non-user	5	1	
Lukole	User	9	7	3
	Non-user	3	2	

Similarly even access to higher education does not explain the difference between the users and non-users of the ICT services.

Table 7.11 gives the number of earning members of the user and non-user families, while Table 7.12 presents their respective economic status.

The number of earning members may not indicate better economic position of the families. Users and non-users show similar pattern for earning members per family (Table 7.11).

Table 7.11: Number of earning members

Villages	Types	One	Two	Three	Four or more
K9	User	5	3		
	Non-user				
Ngara	User	8	5	2	1
	Non-user	3	6	1	
Lukole	User	33	9	4	
	Non-user	30	14		

Table 7.12: Economic status of the families

Villages	Types of respondent	Higher income	Middle income	Lower income
K9	User		Mainly	
	Non-user		Mainly	
Ngara	User		Mainly	
	Non-user		Mainly	
Lukole	User		Mainly	
	Non-user		Mainly	

The respondent families are from middle-income group. This classification refers to the relative economic position in the region, and not any general economic standard.

In general, ICT services are accessed mainly by the people in service sector, and rarely by people from any other occupation. The users want the MCT to provide multiple services including sell, maintenance, repair of PC and other accessories, training, etc. The non-users mostly talk about the lack of familiarity of the services.

Observations on MCTs in Tanzania

The MCTs provide services to the socially and economically uprooted people of the refugee camps. The issues here are different from other cases. The MCTs in this case, address humanitarian needs and as such arguments for society or community oriented programme are out of place. Social and economic fabric being torn, services have to be individual oriented and run under close cooperation with various national and international agencies. Having very little economic base, social interaction is the main purpose of the use of the ICT services.

Summary and Conclusions

Summary

Based on the studies of six cases of the community access project of ITU, we proposed to present an understanding on how to make ICT contribute to social and economic development. It began with a brief theoretical contour on the relationship between information and development. It has been broadly postulated that a marginal economy (in other words in a rural and remote area) can also be distinguished from a developed economy in terms of the nature and extent of information use, which becomes more complex as an economy progresses from a simple subsistence economy to one that is diversified and integrated into the global economy. We have argued that in the process of this transformation, a community centric marginal economy graduates to a proliferation of individual enterprises.

To achieve the transformation, like many other developmental programmes, there have to be planned efforts to prepare the people of a marginal economy to ensure that they are ICT-ready. One way of handling this preparation is to create community-based access to ICT services. The ICT, however, is only a tool. To make it useful, access to ICT has to come with other social and economic development programmes like, universal education, skill development, infrastructure development and also programmes that create economic opportunities.

Six community access projects were studied with this broad understanding. The types of cases chosen provided an opportunity to compare at least four cases at different stages of economic and social development. These were projects in Mali, Bhutan, Honduras and Vietnam i.e. from projects located in a marginal economy to those in a fast growing economy of Vietnam. In this study we have not tried to find out or establish any relationship between ICT uses and development. Instead, theoretical understanding has been used to highlight the ways of making information and ICT a part of the developmental process of these regions. The MCTs in Nicaragua and Tanzania provide additional perspectives on the link between the use of ICT and stages of economic development. Table 8.1 presents the broad economic characteristics and MCT performance in these six countries.

Table 8.1: Comparative status of the MCTs

MCTs in	State of economy of the villages around MCT	Literacy	Services Target to	Services Accessed by	Cost-revenue balance
Mali	Marginal economy	Poor	Individual	Individual	Achieved
Bhutan	Less developed	Good	Individual/ community	Individual	Not achieved
Honduras	Developing	Very good	Individual	Individual	Achieved
Vietnam	Fast developing	Excellent	Individual/ community	Individual	Not achieved
Nicaragua	Developing	Very Good	Programme of health and disaster management	Govt. admn.	NA
Tanzania	Less developed	Very good	Individual	Individual	NA

Mali

The MCT projects at Timbuctu in Mali shows the reach of the ITU initiatives. Although for centuries it remained the part of ancient trading route, the town of Timbuctu and the small villages around it (nearest is 9 km away) were largely untouched by modern infrastructure and economic activities. Out of the three closest villages (that were studied for the present purpose) around the MCT, the farthest one is 52 km away and has 9 households dependent on traditional handicrafts for livelihood. The literacy rate of the villages varies from 18 to 5%, and it is 60% in the town of Timbuctu. Electricity is rare in the villages. The use of MCT is restricted to the people in Timbuctu town. The town itself is predominantly agriculture (age old) dependent with some household units engaged in traditional artisan crafts and commercial activities around those crafts. The case of MCT in Mali does not question the efficacy of the programme of carrying ICT to Timbuctu. On the contrary, it suggests that the clue to sustainability of MCTs has to be looked in such extreme cases as well. After the project period was over in 2002, MCT services have been auctioned to a private operator for a monthly return to the project. Is the question of sustainability resolved in the case of MCT at Timbuctu? An answer to the question has to take in to account the fact that the remote and rural areas around the MCT at Timbuctu remained largely untouched by ICT.

Bhutan

Like Mali, Bhutan also presents another extreme case of ICT isolation. Large part of this tiny Himalayan kingdom, dotted with small hamlets, is inaccessible to modern modes of communications. The existing postal network, (as it has been done in case of Vietnam) run by Bhutan Post has been used to reach the remotest part of the country. With the spread of education (a major government initiative) among younger generation, the excitement was visible when school results were made available through Internet. It is strongly believed that with appropriate content development the access worthiness of the ICT services would enhance the sustainability. Sustainability question not withstanding, the spread of education has brought a discernible change in ICT usage of the common people in Bhutan. In the interaction, the users of ICT facilities were unambiguous in telling about the kind of services they needed.

Honduras

The villages studied in Honduras have relatively high rate of literacy around 70%–80% varying with the remoteness and prosperity of the villages. The MCTs here show a revenue surplus over the running cost. From the use pattern of the MCTs in Honduras, it is clear that a large cross-section of the population in the area use MCT services. Over the years children and population in the age group of 15–40 (that are expected to be ICT-friendly) have emerged as important users of services, particularly, telephone and Internet. As expected, the telephone is the most important of all ICT services. Internet is also a frequently used service. The latter is due to significant dependence of the villagers on remittances of family members living and working abroad.

The MCTs in Honduras are different from those in Vietnam in more than one way. Unlike the observations in Vietnam, the ICT use pattern in Honduras does not distinctly differ between user and non-user groups. In fact, the economic, social and demographic positions of the households in both the groups are quite similar. The economy of the villages around the MCTs is pre-dominantly agriculture with a small section of household based industries in some cases. General economic conditions being poor and economic activities lacking diversity, the need for ICT services is quite dormant. Although MCTs have attained some surplus over the operational cost, the concept of MCT has not become a national mission as it has happened in Vietnam. The MCTs in rural areas are being run by the local community on revenue sharing basis.

Vietnam

In Vietnam the government has a clearly defined policy of making ICT available universally. The 'cultural points' have become the nodal points for reaching the villages. This, coupled with the policy of universal education and the expansion of economic activities through industrialization, has created the necessary objective condition for the foundation of demand for ICT. Another important dimension has been the gradual transformation from a society that was being fed with perceived need of information, to a society where younger generations search for information of their needs and choice. This transformation has far reaching implications on the development of the market for information. In the emerging market, the types and nature of the demand for information would be multi-faceted and autonomous, and the supply of services would be governed by the emerging characteristics of the burgeoning demand. The user and non-user survey is unambiguous about the fact that: (i) ICT use extends with the expansion of the economic activities and infrastructure development, and (ii) it also shows strong positive correlations with the educational status of the families.

Nicaragua

The Nicaragua project is different from other projects. The project is dedicated to a specific programme of extending health/medical services as well as disaster prevention, relief and management. Under the project, the central health administration system is connected with the local health centres for data communication. While in the other projects, the purpose of use of services is left to the individual users, in case of Nicaragua project, people benefit specifically from the efficient health/disaster-related information available to the local health centres. The project is a part of the government programme to harmonize and reinforce the vigilance systems of the public health.

The benefits of the project are considered as public good and are available cost-free to the villagers. Hence the user and non-user survey was not carried out. Instead, we present the socio-economic profiles of the remote and rural areas which are connected with the network created by the project.

Tanzania

The MCTs are located at politically sensitive western border areas of Tanzania. The project aims at providing ICT-based information and communication services to refugee camps in order to increase the access to medical information, access to peacekeeping and conflict resolution, and for the integration of displaced communities into local and global opportunities. The uniqueness of MCTs in Tanzania is not only in terms of services to be provided, but also the target communities, which are socially and economically destabilised. Being socially and economically uprooted, refugee camps have given uniformity to the social and economic lives of the residents of the camps.

Conclusions

The journey from the communes in Vietnam to the refugee camps in Tanzania, via sleepy hamlets in the Himalayan terrains of Bhutan and ancient Timbuctu in Mali with a detour to aspiring Nicaragua and Honduras has witnessed that the community access projects have touched a wide spectrum of social and economic aspects of rural and remoteness across the globe. The impact of the projects is as varied as the socio-political states.

One of the most important findings of the study is the interplay between the two sets of factors influencing spread of ICT use. Literacy, number of school going children, number of children going for higher education, number of members in the ICT-friendly age group etc have positive influence on the use of ICT. On the other hand, a lack of economic diversity and enterprise, a dependence on traditional economic occupation and an overall lack of economic opportunities are deterrents to ICT use. The study brings out that, while in the case of Vietnam two set of factors were moving in the same direction creating a positive influence, for Honduras the positive effect of the first set of factors has been outweighed by the negative impact of the second set.

In the case of Vietnam, although only four MCTs have been established in two districts, enthusiasm of the government has spread the idea in a scaled-down version to all communes across the country through the 'cultural points', each serving eight to ten villages. There are an increasing number of users of MCT services in Vietnam. However, MCTs are yet to attain cost-revenue balance. That was not a deterrent for a determined government to implement the idea at every corner of the country. Almost 100% literacy coupled with large-scale investment for development of social and physical infrastructure and fast industrialization has created the foundation for emerging information society. The MCT pilot project in Vietnam has been visualized as hub of information services, business support centre, educational services, tele-medicine, etc. Development of appropriate application modules got delayed for several reasons. The upcoming information society of Vietnam is expected to see many private initiatives assessing the changing needs and developing appropriate application modules independent of MCTs. The MCT pilot project and the extension of the idea nation-wide has been instrumental in the emergence of Vietnam model of the emerging information society.

In Bhutan, due to the small size of the country, the Post Office Telekiosk project could cover the whole postal network across Bhutan. The economy of Bhutan is not as vibrant as that of Vietnam, but the spread of education among younger generation of Bhutan has created new enthusiasm about ICT. The telekiosks, located at post offices, are triggering this enthusiasm that does not find match due to lack of diversity in economic activities, poor infrastructure and negligible industrialisation. Therefore the nature of demand for ICT services is less individualistic and more community service based. As our survey of users and non-users has revealed, students, farmers, and other villagers ask for services that would provide them information on education, agriculture, health, government programmes, etc. The project authorities in Bhutan have already taken steps in this regard. Being operated through post offices, the telekiosks could minimize the operational cost of the project to match the nominal revenue generating potential. Meeting cost-revenue balance is a distant possibility in case of Bhutan project, although it has overwhelming influence in Bhutanese society.

On the contrary MCTs in Honduras show a positive revenue balance over the cost and hence positive sustainability. Being managed by local communities, MCTs in Honduras come closer to the Vietnam model. The similarity, however, ends there. The MCTs in Vietnam, although do not earn enough revenue over the operational cost, are widely replicated across the country through active government initiatives. In the case of Honduras, sustainability is largely due to the needs of the families who have members settled abroad, and families are largely dependent on the remittances. There are not many government initiatives for replication of the project.

The telekiosk in Timbuctu has been auctioned to a private party for a monthly rent. Therefore the revenue from the project has been assured. The services provided by telekiosks are targeted to individuals. The villages around telekiosks are too remote and poor to be the source of revenue for telekiosk. The main clients, therefore, are from the town of Timbuctu. It appears that, to reach the ICT have-nots of the villages around the MCTs as we have seen in the case of Bhutan, the services may need to be oriented to communities instead of individuals.

Nicaragua offers an alternative model to the Vietnam model. The MCTs in Nicaragua are oriented towards a particular programme for health administration and disaster management. Therefore, it is neither an individual oriented service nor targeted to a particular community; it aims to serve a cause for overall societal benefits. The question of cost-revenue balance does not arise in this case, as individuals are not charged for use, and the costs are covered as part of a health care budget.

The MCTs in the refugee camps of Tanzania are to serve a humanitarian cause. The camps are run by international agencies. The MCTs are part of international initiative to provide relief to the refugees.

Table 8.1 summarizes the salient aspects of the MCTs discussed above. It appears from Table 8.1 that the MCT project needs to distinguish, right at the beginning, about the orientation of its services. The orientation has to be decided based on the state of the economy and the literacy status of the area. These two have emerged as the most important factors for creation of an information society. The conflict between target and service is apparent from the Table. In case of Vietnam, given the overall state of development and high literacy rate, an individual-oriented programme would be effective. This probably explains the reluctance to develop application module as it was envisaged in the original programme. It appears that such community-targeted programme became redundant in case of Vietnam. On the contrary, in case of Bhutan, the present state of economy does not make a case for individual-targeted programme. The demand from the newly emerging educated people is for a community-targeted programme. Although there has been no such demand from Timbuctu, the argument for Bhutan also holds good here. Another important aspect is revealed from the Table 8.1 is regarding self-sustainability of MCTs. Two MCT projects (Honduras and Mali) that have shown positive revenue balance over cost are those having individual oriented services, and mostly earned revenue by providing services that could pay. The MCT in Mali is a case where individual oriented programme should be replaced by community-oriented programme to reach the remotest and poorest of the populace. Overall, it appears that for the cause of remote and rural areas a Nicaragua type of model would be more effective, whereas an individual-oriented but community-managed model would more appropriate for upcoming economies like Vietnam.

The study draws following broad conclusions

(i) Access to ICT has to be seen in the context of access to information and its implication on social and economic transformation of a region. It means, in other words, that ICT cannot stand alone to contribute to the development initiatives. Since information is accessed for making social and economic decisions, there has to be enabling social and economic opportunities to make access to information useful.

(ii) The study brings out that education, both basic literacy and higher education, is the most important enabling factor that makes access to information useable by the target group of people. It also shows two contrasting cases, where in one case, literacy and economic opportunities make communities ICT friendly, while in the other lack of economic opportunities results to limited use of ICT even in the presence of high literacy rate. In other words, the study indicates that ICT itself will not bring any significant change in the economic and social status of the marginal economies.

Conversely, developmental initiatives are not likely to realise their fruits if they are not integrated with access to ICT. The study, therefore, suggests that the access to ICT programmes have to be taken up as an integral part of the other ongoing developmental projects.

(iii) The bench level study that is generally carried out before implementation of the programme aiming to provide access to ICT programme, has to focus more on the possibilities of integrating ICT with the other developmental programmes, than the existing socio-economic status of the target region. Literacy status of the target community being the fundamental factor behind the success of such projects. The ICT programmes either have to target high literacy regions, or have to become part of spread of literacy programmes.

(iv) The question of sustainability is misplaced. It is too early to consider the access to information as a business proposal, that too for the economies/societies which have very little felt-need for information. It is also too early to think of making profit from selling and buying information and related services. The study suggests that the social rate of return from the access to information is likely to be very high, and ignoring it for the sake of cost-revenue balance would be self-defeating. The study also suggests that the access to information, on the contrary, has to be taken up as an investment that has overarching impact on all activities of an economy, and therefore, cannot and should not be constricted by money return in the short-run.

(v) For evaluation of the ICT projects, most important aspect is to examine the extent of integration of the project activities with the other developmental programmes including spread of literacy. Suitable proxies for this purpose have to be developed separately project-wise. Indicative proxies are: number of contents based on developmental programmes, accessible through ICT access points; number of times such contents being accessed; number of individuals accessing these contents etc.

(vi) As postulated in the study, the expected impacts of the access to information, when it is coupled with access to education and economic opportunities, are: growth of individual enterprises, diversification of economic and social activities, and also growth of export and import in the target regions. These can be used as indictors to monitor the impact of the extensive access to information through ICT.

Bibliography

1. Anderson, J. et al. (1999), *Applying the lessons of Participatory Communication and Training to rural Telecentres*, FAO, July.
2. Barber, P. and N. Cutinet (2001), *Measuring the digital economy: US and European perspectives*. STAR Issue Report No. 2, ENST: Paris.
3. Barlow, J.P. (1998), *Africa Rising: Everything you know about Africa is wrong*, Wired, Jan.
4. Brown, M. M. (2001), *Can ICTs Address the needs of the Poor?: A Commentary from UNDP*, June.
5. Cassan, M. (1997), *Information and Organization: A new perspective on the theory of firm*, Clarendon Press, Oxford.
6. Castells, M. (1998), *The Information Age*, Vols. 1, 2 & 3, Blackwell, Oxford, UK.
7. Castells, M. (1999), 'Information Technology, Globalization and Social Development.' Paper prepared for the UNRISD Conference on Information Technology and Social Development, Geneva, Sep. 1999.
8. Chowdhury, N. (2000), *Poverty Alleviation and Information/ Communication Technologies*, www.eb2000.org/shortnote19.htm
9. Colle, Royal and Raul Roman (1999), *Communication Centers and Developing Nations*. Http://www.devmedia.org/document/ Banga.htm
10. Daly, J.A. (1999), *A Conceptual Framework for the Study of the Impacts of the Internet*. Center for International Development and Conflict Management, University of Maryland: MD.

11. Duncombe, R. and R. Heeks (1999), *Information ICTs and Small Enterprise: Findings from Botswana,* IDPM Manchester Working Paper No. 7, November.
12. Ernberg, Johan (1998), "Telecommunications for sustainable development". In Don Richardson (ed.), *The first mile of connectivity*. FAO, Rome.
13. Ernberg, Johan (1998a), Integrated Rural Development and Universal Access: Towards a framework for evaluation of Multipurpose Community Telecentre Pilot projects implemented by ITU and its partners. ITU, Geneva.
14. Figueres, J.M. (2003), Preface in, A. Badshah et al (eds.), *Connected for Development: Information Kiosks and Sustainability,* U.N. ICT Task Force Series 4, New York.
15. Fuchs, Richard (1998), "Little Engines that Did" - Case Histories from the Global Telecentre Movement. IDRC, Ottawa. http://www.idrc.ca/acacia/engine/index.html
16. Gomez, R., P. Hunt and E. Lamoureux (1999), *Telecentre Evaluation and Research: a global perspective*. Report of an International Meeting on Telecentre Evaluation September 28–30th 1999. International Development Research Centre, Canada.
17. Heeks, R. (1999), *Information and Communication Technologies, Poverty and Development*, IDPM Manchester, Development Informatics Working Paper Series, No. 5, June.
18. Hudson, H.E. (1984), *When Telephone Reach the Village: The Role of Telecommunications in Rural Development*, Norwood, NJ.
19. Hudson, H.E. (2001), *The Potential of ICTs for Development: Opportunities and Obstacles*, Telecommunication Management and Policy Program, Unversity of Sanfrancisco, www.usfca.edu/facstaff/hudson.
20. Neto, I., C. Kenny, S. Janakiram and C. Watt (2005), "Look Before You Leap: The bumpy road to E-development", in R. Schware (ed), *E-development: From excitement to efficiency, World Bank*, Washington DC.
21. Jarboe, K.P. (2001), *Inclusion in the Information Age: Reframing the Debate*. Athena Alliance: Washington D.C.
22. Kanfi, Shady and Frank Tulus (1998), *Acacia: What is a telecentre?. On CentraTEL*, British Council, Johannesburg.

23. Latchman, C. and D. Walker (eds.) (2001), *Telecentres: Case Studies and Key Issues,* Vancouver: Commonwealth of Learning. www.col.org/telecentres
24. Lanvin, B. (2003), Foreword in, A. Badshah et al (eds.), *Connected for Development: Information Kiosks and Sustainability,* U.N. ICT Task Force Series 4, New York.
25. Leontev, A.N. (1978), *Activity, Consciousness and Personality.* Prentice Hall: New Jersey
26. Leontev A.N. (1981), *Problems of the Development of the Mind.* Progress Publishers, Moscow
27. McConnell, Paul (ed.) (1995), *Making a Difference: Measuring the Impact of Informaiton on Development.* International Development Research centre, Ottawa Canada.
28. Michiels, S.I. and L. Van Crowder, (2001), *Discovering the 'Magic Box': Local Appropriation of Information and Communication Technologies (ICTs).* Communication for Development Group, Extension, Education and Communication Service, FAO. Rome, May 2001.
29. Mansell, R. and U. When (eds.) (1998), *Knowledge Societies: Information Technology for Sustainable Development,* OUP
30. Moyo, L.M. (1996), *Information Technology Strategies for Africa's Survival in the Twenty-first Century: IT all Pervasive,* Information Technology for Development, Vol. 7, No. 1.
31. Opoku-Mensah, Aida (1998), *Telecentres Excite Ugandans - but what about the poor? Panos News,* August 1998. http://www.oneworld.org/panos/news
32. Okpaku, J.O. (2006), "Leapfrogging into the Information Economy: Harnessing information and communication technologies in Botswana, Mauritania, and Tanzania", in L. Fox and R. Liebenthal (eds.), *Attacking African Poverty: Experience from the ground,* World Bank, Washington DC.
33. Richardson, Don (ed.) (1998), *The first mile of connectivity.* FAO, Rome.
34. Richardson, Don (2002), *Towards Universal Telecom Access for Rural and Remote Communities,* www.telecommons .com
35. Roman, R. and R. Colle (2003), "Notes on Research for Telecentre Development", in A. Badshah et al (eds.), *Connected*

for Development: Information Kiosks and Sustainability, U.N. ICT Task Force Series 4, New York.

36. Samarajiva, R. and A. Zainudeen (2008), *ICT Infrastructure in Emerging Asia: Policy and Regulatory roadblocks*, Sage, New Delhi.
37. Schware, R. (2005), *E-development: From excitement to efficiency*, World Bank, Washington DC.
38. Simon, H.A. (1957), *Models of Man*, New York, John Wiley.
39. Valadez, J. and R. Duran (2007), "Redefining the Digital Divide: Beyond access to computers and the Internet", *The High School Journal*, 90(3), 31–44.
40. Wresch, W. (1996), *Disconnected: Haves and Have-Nots in the Information Age*, New Brunswick, Rutgers University Press.
41. Orbicom-IDRC, (2008), *Digital Review of Asia Pacific 2007–2008*, Sage, New Delhi.
42. O'Neil, D. (2001), *Merging Theory with Practice: Toward an Evaluation Framework for Community Informatics*. School of Public Policy, Georgia Institute of Technology, Georgia.
43. Warschauer, M. (2002), "Reconceptualizing the Digital Divide", *First Monday* 7(7).
44. Warschauer, M. (2003), *Technology and Social Inclusion: Rethinking the digital divide*, Cambridge, MA: The MIT Press.
45. Zjip, W. (1994), *Improving the Transfer and Use of Agricultural Information: A Guide to Information Technology*. World Bank Discussion Paper 247, The World Bank, Washington.
46. Zembylas, M. (2009), "ICT for Development and Social Justice: Some theoretical Issues", in C. Vrasidas, M. Zembylas, G.V. Glass, (eds.), *ICT for Development and Social Justice*, CARDET.
47. Zembylas, M. and C. Vrasidas (2005), "Globalization, Information and Communication Technologies, and the prospect of a Global Village: Promise of inclusion or electronic colonization?", *Journal of Curriculum Studies*, 37(1), 65–84.
48. Zongo, Gaston (1999), *What is a telecentre? A review of best practice and models*. Paper at the Building the Information Community in Africa, February.

Index